how to start a home-based
Public Relations Business

how to start a home-based

Public Relations Business

Randi Minetor

gpp®

Guilford, Connecticut

Editorial Director: Cynthia Hughes Cullen
Editor: Tracee Williams
Project Editor: Lauren Brancato
Text Design: Sheryl P. Kober
Layout: Sue Murray

ISSN 2165-9230
ISBN 978-0-7627-7343-5

Printed in the United States of America
10 9 8 7 6 5 4 3 2 1

To Adele Fico, who showed me the ropes and taught me that "down" was just a precursor to "on top."

To Gary Stockman, who turned me on to the active voice.

And to the late Audrey Saphar, who spared me nothing and taught me everything.

Contents

Acknowledgments

Many, many thanks to Cynthia Hughes, Tracee Williams, Lauren Brancato, and the team at Globe Pequot Press for their work in bringing this book to fruition. As always, I thank my wonderful agent, Regina Ryan, for all that she does to keep my writing career on track, from her advocacy for me with publishers to the new opportunities she discovers.

I made many new friends in the public relations industry and deepened some old friendships while working on this book. In particular, I am indebted to Amy Blum, Georgi Bohrod, Elise Brown, Christopher Budd, Sally Cohen, Lindsey Gardner, Barbara Haig, Elliott Stares, Micah Warren, and Anjani Webb for the time they spent with me, for the remarkable insights they shared, and for their candidness in telling the stories of their fascinating careers.

Finally, no book project would be worthwhile or any fun at all were it not for my husband, Nic Minetor, whose bottomless well of encouragement brings abundance and light to even the darkest days. If I lead a charmed life, it's because of his place in it.

Introduction

Your work is going to fill a large part of your life, and the only way to be truly satisfied is to do what you believe is great work. And the only way to do great work is to love what you do. If you haven't found it yet, keep looking. Don't settle. As with all matters of the heart, you'll know when you find it. And, like any great relationship, it just gets better and better as the years roll on. So keep looking until you find it. Don't settle.

—Steve Jobs in his commencement address at Stanford University, June 2005

Why am I the right person to tell you how to start your own home-based public relations business?

As I write this, my own business, Minetor & Company, Inc., is beginning its fourteenth fiscal year. My corporate headquarters fills a 120-square-foot room on the second floor of my 1917 American Foursquare–style home, and the carefully restored American chestnut trim around the windows and doors is nicely offset by walls painted a rich shade of sage. Outside my window, Baltimore orioles sing as they plunder our hummingbird feeders, and eastern chipmunks emerge from holes hidden in our gardens to chase one another across the yard.

No one will interrupt my writing time with the demand that I attend a meeting to discuss: "Who are we as a company, and what do we mean by public relations?" No feuding graphic artists will bring their personal squabbles to my office door, and no looming threat of an end-of-year layoff will gnaw at the edges of my concentration.

Perhaps you're reading this book because you now face the struggle I did: the fear of cutting the cord and floating free of the corporate life, without the security of a dependable paycheck or a comfortable benefits package. Perhaps you're a solid PR account executive and copywriter, and you've suddenly sat back and considered the vast field of potential clients who could benefit from your expertise, knowing full well that some of these exciting smaller companies cannot afford your agency's fees.

Or perhaps you're a journalist with a lower salary than you deserve, and you know that the PR people who come to you with story pitches are probably paid 50 to 75 percent more than you. You may think of them as "flacks" today, but those PR professionals are charging three-digit hourly fees to their clients . . . and with your first-hand media experience, you know you could pitch more effectively than they can.

Is it time for you to sever the ties and form your own public relations business? This book will help you make that decision, with worksheets, tools, and frank discussions about the life of the independent practitioner.

In this book, I'll share my experience with what works, what you should avoid, and what you really need to know to build your own PR business successfully. I'll talk about setting up your office, finding and keeping clients, the ups and downs of working at home, and management of your reputation as well as your client list. Perhaps most important, I'll discuss some of the profession-specific ethical issues you may face, and some strategies for dealing with unavoidable (and avoidable) errors, botched news conferences, "loose cannon" clients, dangling retainers, and—worst of all—the ones who want you to lie.

Are you ready to think about your next big adventure? Let's get started!

01 | So You Want to Start a Public Relations Business

Chances are good that you've picked up this book because you are already employed as a public relations (PR) or journalism professional. Maybe you're hip-deep in the sweeping industry changes that have made PR folks some of the most influential people in the world of modern media.

Today's PR professionals have risen above the days when we spent hours phoning the newsroom and begging a reporter to take an interest in a story—a practice that earned us the derogatory nickname "flack." Today PR people are respected as slick political operatives, integral members of a celebrity's entourage, and gatekeepers to the critical information editors and producers need to fill a twenty-four-hour news cycle and tens of thousands of websites.

Today 277 colleges offer public relations majors—literally hundreds more than thirty years ago, when I began graduate school—while the US Department of Labor reports that jobs in public relations are "expected to increase faster than the average for all occupations through 2014, spurred by intense domestic and global competition in products and services offered to consumers." Equity firm Veronis Suhler Stevenson reports that the annual compound growth rate in PR jobs was 10.3 percent from 2006 through 2011.

There's never been a better time to be a PR professional—and if you're in tune with the needs of today's media, you have a talent for filtering out the lame story ideas to find the ones that will make editors' eyes gleam, and you've kept pace with the technological revolution that has replaced journalism with social networking, then you've positioned yourself to be a leader in this marketplace.

Your skills may mean that you will never be unemployed . . . but traditional employment may have lost its luster for you. Working in a corporate PR department or a big communications firm no longer carries the promises of a fat paycheck and long-term employment. When corporations announce layoffs, often the communications department tops the downsizing list. More PR people than ever choose the corporate route to gain experience and a professional network early on, and then leave to form their own businesses when the time is right.

Why PR Now?

Not since the invention of television have we seen such a metamorphosis in the way news travels to the consumer. Cable news channels struggle to fill twenty-four hours of uninterrupted time daily with information, reportage, commentary, and speculation. Citizen journalism now garners almost as much respect and interest as professional news, with the average person's ability to capture video of a major event with a mobile phone and post it to Facebook, Twitter, and YouTube in seconds. Wars, natural disasters, conflicts within borders blocked to conventional journalism, and celebrity scandals of every flavor now get reported by college students armed with Flip cameras and tablet computers.

This communications revolution extends well beyond national politics and international news, to the bread-and-butter trade media relations that we perform for business-to-business clients. Today every magazine in every niche market, from caskets to municipal water distribution, has a digital edition distributed by e-mail, a website where editors post news releases, online forums for end-user participation in discussions about products and applications, and blogs by experts in each field. Companies with industrial products now maintain Facebook pages and post their activities on Twitter. The days of striving for a page in a trade magazine's print edition are coming to an end . . . and most important for our purposes, clients are desperate to become part of the online conversation.

The smart PR practitioner can capitalize on this opportunity to guide clients into the social networking age. The savvy, independent PR business owner can offer cost-effective services that allow companies of any size to be all over the web, boosting their company's position on Google searches and generating lots of website hits.

This is the world you're about to enter as a new PR business owner. There's never been a better time to start your own PR firm—if you've kept up with the technology and the skills required to straddle the traditional and the new in today's media.

Some Basic Assumptions about You

In framing this book, I've made some assumptions about your background in public relations—specifically, that you actually have experience in the field.

This book is for people who are already working in PR, either as a public relations practitioner or as a journalist. *How to Start a Home-based Public Relations Business* will help you create your company, providing the information you need to establish your company as an entity, gather the right tools, assemble a comfortable home office, find and attract clients, price your services, get paid, pay your taxes, keep your clients for the long term, and maintain your reputation (that thing the folks on the marketing side call your "brand identity") as a skilled, scrupulously ethical business owner.

Let me be clear here: This is not a book about how to do public relations. While the information I provide is germane specifically to the issues a PR business can and will face, this is not a primer to the profession. If you have no background or experience at all in public or media relations, I highly recommend that you join the Public Relations Society of America chapter in your area (the list of chapters can be found at www.prsa.org) and take advantage of every skill session and mentoring opportunity offered there. If you're just graduating from college and you want to start your own PR business, take at least a year and find an internship in a respected PR agency, or in the corporate communications department of a large corporation or nonprofit organization. You will need this experience to build a portfolio and convince prospective clients that you have the skills they need, and that you know what you're doing in the field.

Why I Started Minetor & Company, Inc.

For me, no perfect storm of circumstances or blinding flash of insight told me that it was time to sever the ties with Saphar & Associates, the most respected PR firm in Rochester, New York, in the late 1990s, where I was a vice president. Instead, the day came at the end of a three-year series of events, beginning with the sudden death of my mentor and employer, Audrey Saphar, in a one-car accident when she was just fifty-four years old. The agency rallied and we remained in fine business standing with Audrey's husband, Ed Saphar, at the helm . . . but a nagging thought took hold in the back of my mind. Audrey had died so young, and so unexpectedly. This could happen to anyone. *It could happen to me.*

Meanwhile, the way the world did business took an astonishing turn. The Internet changed everything, from the methods through which we communicated to the way we bought merchandise. This thrilling new technology seemed shrouded in mystery to those of us who had barely mastered the word processor. Start-up companies sprang up to develop and market application services, connectivity structures, hardware platforms, software for the home and office, and untold thousands of other products. Every meeting with a new client evolved into a breathless discussion about where the World Wide Web was going next.

The final factor came from an unlikely place: a sales training course I attended with several Saphar colleagues. Offered by the Professional Sales Institute—which has since become 2logical, a worldwide leadership and sales training company—the classroom work included an exercise in which we compared various qualities that were important in our lives, to determine which were truly our highest priorities. Much like the NCAA's March Madness brackets, the exercise asked (and I'm paraphrasing here), "Which is more important to you: Status or security? Financial freedom or recognition?" and so on, until just two qualities survived every matchup. To my amazement, the things I thought I valued most highly—security, power, and a steady paycheck—fell off the list in the first round. My remaining most valued aspects: independence and self-leadership!

I tendered my resignation from Saphar & Associates the next day. Three months later, I drew my first paycheck from Minetor & Company. And after years of determining my most effective and profitable niches, the best matches for my skills, and the kinds of projects that make me spring out of bed in the morning, I have a roster of clients in manufacturing, professional services, elder care, and community college education. Together, these provide the income I need to share support of my household with my husband, lighting designer/photographer Nic Minetor, and feed our passion for travel to America's national parks. It also affords me the flexibility to write books like this one (*How to Start a Home-based Public Relations Business* is my twenty-first commercially published book).

What circumstances have motivated you to pick up this book? What's happening in your work and personal life that triggered your interest in working for yourself? If you've read this far, it may be time for you to look closely at your own situation, and think about the many benefits of working for yourself as a trusted PR representative for the clients that interest you most. Best of all, it's time to look at that hourly fee your agency employer charges clients for your time . . . and think about all that money going into your own business's bank account.

Working from Home Is "The New Black"

There was a time, not so long ago, when business owners of all stripes worried that working from home would make us look small, weak, and under-resourced. Clients once believed that people working from home were actually unemployed and struggling to make ends meet, so we would take whatever small projects they tossed to us, and we'd be grateful for the work. Freelancing meant that clients could hire us on the cheap, with some believing that they could deal with us on an under-the-table, off-the-record basis.

Our choice to work at home seemed a signal to some clients that we were not serious about our business, or that we had some other motive for leaving the golden handcuffs of corporate or agency leadership behind. In my earliest days as Minetor & Company, some clients asked me if I was having a baby, or if I had young kids at home. "No kids?" they'd say. "Then why are you staying home?"

We can be thankful today that the world of business transformed so completely since the turn of the twenty-first century. Working from home is now a respected means of doing business, practiced as telecommuting by corporation-employed professionals, and as freelancing by sole-proprietor business owners.

Why the shift in perception of the at-home business? First and foremost, more people now work from home than ever before. The US Department of Labor tells us that in 2004, 19.5 million people worked in home-based businesses. In 2010, the US Census discovered that thirty-eight million people ran businesses out of their homes. Some of this growth undoubtedly springs from the 2008 economic crash and the subsequent struggle to find traditional employment, but with this hardship comes a level of self-evaluation and soul-searching—and the resulting insights spur people to take chances to achieve their dreams of self-employment and business ownership.

Beyond the economy, home-based businesses have gained a level of acknowledgment and respect from clients of all sizes and market niches. Clients now understand that home-based businesses can offer them lower rates than our agency counterparts, because we do not carry the monumental overhead of a stand-alone office, a bottom-heavy support staff, or a lengthy approval stream for each project.

Often the chief executive officer, chief marketing officer, or corporate spokesperson in a major corporation prefers to build a working relationship with a specific practitioner, rather than hiring a whole agency and working with an ever-changing account team. These high-ranking professionals understand that when they work with a home-based business owner, they will always reach "the boss"—that's you—when they need your services. This is especially important if speechwriting is part of your skill set, as top-level executives form relationships that last for decades with speechwriters who know their industry, their voice, their presentation style, and their favorite message points.

Perhaps most important, many smaller companies appreciate the option of working with a home-based vendor who understands the issues a small organization faces. As a business owner, you have the opportunity to connect with a client on an entirely new and different level, addressing the issues that affect their company's image beyond their most recent news release. The more solidly you can cement relationships when your clients are small, the more satisfying—and profitable—that relationship will become as these clients' businesses grow and prosper. Working on an owner-to-owner basis is a completely different experience from the client/account executive relationship, because the client understands that you alone own the responsibility for your company's performance. If the project fails, you fail as well—so, implicitly, you have a much greater stake in success than you did when you worked for someone else's agency or corporation.

From the Field

Elise Brown, Drummer PR

"People just started calling me."

"I was not planning on working for myself," said Elise Brown, president and CEO of Drummer PR in Philadelphia, Pennsylvania. "I really like in-house PR, and I didn't think I'd work well as a solo practitioner. I said I was going to take a break. But people just started calling me."

It's no wonder that clients sought out Brown's remarkable skills and experience. Her weighty portfolio includes the promotional know-how that put Ben & Jerry's Ice Cream on the national map, combining her experience as a radio disc jockey with her PR savvy to launch the company's bestselling flavor, Cherry Garcia.

That achievement would have some PR professionals resting on their laurels, but Brown followed this with promotion of the New Jersey State Aquarium (now the Adventure Aquarium), establishment of a new recording and video label for the QVC home shopping network, and several years as the senior manager of

---

feature content and, later, senior PR manager and director of public relations for Sirius Satellite Radio.

It sounds like a dream career—and it has been—but the day came when Brown had had enough of commuting to Rockefeller Center, first from Philadelphia and then from central New Jersey. "I had lived through 9/11, I had lived through the blackout of 2003, and I was completely fried," she said. "My work was way too much without enough support staff. The commute had become unbearable, and so had I. I was making big New York money, but at some point it's just not worth it."

With her wedding on the horizon, Brown took the advice of her fiancé, Patrick Berkery: "He said, 'Why don't you just take some time off?'" She planned an idyllic six months or so of wedding festivities, gardening, and kicking back . . . until the phone began to ring.

"People would call and say, 'What are you doing? Could you do this little job for me?' I helped with promoting an album, and some other small jobs. Then one of the big radio personalities at Sirius called me and said, 'Can I hire you as my personal publicist?' The checks started coming in every month."

Before she knew it, Brown was running a going concern out of a spare bedroom in her home, with clients including a new Internet radio company and a firm that recycles electronics. "I love working with entrepreneurs," she said. "My specialty is people who have something new and different. In the last couple of years, I've worked with a lot of authors—I love to work with them on their first book. They know that I can get them into a realm that covers music as well as the book world."

Her husband came through once again as she considered the name of her company. "I didn't want to be just another PR firm named after a woman," she explained. "I wanted something asexual. While I was thinking about it, my husband [who is a professional musician] was banging away on his drums in the basement. I thought, 'Drummer PR!' I liked the idea that everyone marches to his or her own drumbeat."

Brown and her husband moved to Philadelphia in 2011, where she serves clients from a dedicated home office. Eschewing the go-anywhere laptop in favor of a desktop PC, Brown prefers the sense of coming to an office every day, even if her commute takes her just a few steps down the hall. "I still have my old-fashioned calendar with my clients' things highlighted in colors, and a big bulletin board," she said. "I have a really nice desk I got at Pottery Barn, a huge bookshelf, a console, and a three-drawer filing cabinet." Postage supplies, a scanner, a video camera, and a copier/printer/fax machine are always at hand. On and around these office staples are the materials Brown uses regularly: magazines, music business references, style manuals, poetry anthologies, works of classic literature, dictionaries in several languages, and hard copies of all of her clients' products.

"If I were going to give advice to others, it would be to be prepared for a really erratic pay schedule," she said. "I was used to paychecks for so long! And you have to deal with rejection, no response, no interest, and no coverage. On the other hand, having my own business has given me such fulfillment. Any time I've had a client appear in the *New York Times,* that's a good day."

Brown remembers a nonprofit client's surprise recognition of her at a special event. "At the end of the event, they thanked me in front of everyone," she said. "They had a huge bouquet of flowers they wanted to present to me, and I wasn't even in the auditorium! I was out front, working with the TV crew that had arrived. For them to make this special recognition for me was just unbelievably touching. There have been a lot of moments like that."

The Truth about Working Alone

We've begun to touch on one of the most important aspects of working from home: working alone. In your home-based PR business, you alone are responsible for the success or failure of your business. If the project succeeds, you reap all of the benefits. If a project goes wrong, there's no team to share the blame. Your mistakes are yours alone, and you need to be prepared to take full responsibility when an error becomes a detriment to the client.

I'm talking about risk, a term that makes every business owner's pulse quicken. Some PR professionals thrive on the positive stress of taking the risk, while others are far more comfortable with the sure-thing solution. It's intrinsic in the public relations business that some risk is involved every time you reach out to the media or post a blog entry on a client's behalf. When you work alone, however, you will feel the full impact of a misplaced word, a "fact" that turns out to be a lie, or the hidden truth that comes to light because an industrious old-school journalist digs to find the story behind the story.

What is your tolerance for risk? Even if you take the safest route on every project, a day will come when you face an error or a failure, and you must be prepared to take the consequences. It's rare that such an error ends in a lawsuit—we'll talk about errors and omissions insurance in chapter 5—but the severity of the error may lead you to lose a client. Client turnover is a business fact of life, but you will need to be able to stand back and view the issue objectively, determine the damage control required for your client and for your own business, and make the appropriate reparations or decisions about your own reputation.

You thought I was going to talk about the loneliness of the home-based PR professional, didn't you? Working from home can indeed be a solitary life, but the PR business is social by definition. You will be on the phone with journalists, meeting with clients, networking with interested end-users online, and attending meetings and events to meet new prospects for your business. There may be long hours at your desktop writing articles, releases, speeches, and other materials, but even these activities can be portable and performed elsewhere if you need fellow human beings around you in the mid-afternoon. Which brings us to . . .

The Five Best-Kept Secrets about Working from Home

Writing in your pajamas? That's no secret—although it is truly a major benefit of working at home. Here are more benefits that you may not have considered as you determine whether or not a home-based business is for you.

1. **No one can see what you're doing.** Our employed-by-others mentality has us hard-wired to work at every waking moment, and to sit at our desks and look busy when the project is finished and we have nothing more to do. This "look busy" concept is a phenomenon of the corporate office, where we must appear to put in a full eight-hour or nine-hour day, even when we only have five hours' work to complete. We also insist that we must work during the standard business hours established by whatever job we held most recently. All of this is twentieth-century thinking, and it's anathema to the home-based business owner.

Do you do your best work between 5:00 and 8:00 a.m., or are you a night owl who loves to write after dark? You can set the hours you like, so long as you bill enough hours to meet your business's financial goals.

2. **Location is irrelevant.** Mobile phone, e-mail, instant messaging, Skype, and Facebook allow us to keep in contact with editors and clients from anywhere there's cellular, WiFi, 3G, or 4G signal. It's critical that you are reachable, but where you maintain contact is up to you. I have participated in conference calls from roadside rest stops along the New York State Thruway, conducted interviews from a hotel room in West Yellowstone, Montana, and completed expertise articles and news releases from a fruit stand on the edge of the Florida Everglades while slurping a key lime milkshake. Not only do most clients not care where you are as long as the job gets done, many will express their appreciation of your diligence in keeping in contact with them while you're out of the office.

3. **You're as big as you want to be.** If you've been in the PR business for some time, chances are good that you've already built a network of suppliers who can provide services outside of your personal repertoire. If you're a writer who doesn't do graphic design, link up with several designers whose expertise and work style you trust. If you don't do video production, find a production company that you can call on to turn your great public service announcement idea into reality. If you have overflow writing or if a client needs you to monitor any mention of her products or services online, keep a virtual stable of freelance writers and independent support people who specialize in social networking activity and web searches. None of these people are your employees; they are trusted vendors who can act as part of your organization when you need them. This ability to gear up or wind down is an important part of any home-based business—in fact, it's why so many sole proprietorships have "and Associates" in their corporate name.

4. **Laptops and lattes: the anywhere office.** As I write these words, I'm sitting at a Panera Bread location in Brighton, a suburb of Rochester, New York, where the hubbub of lunchtime patronage provides just enough background noise to feel like company. There's no reason to feel confined to a fraction of your home for an entire workday, thanks to the world's near-universal connectivity and the portability of our work tools. Take that big writing job out to your favorite coffee shop or diner and enjoy the change

of venue—which can have a remarkably positive effect on your productivity. If you don't subscribe to the Internet cafe mentality, try sitting out on your own porch or deck, or pack up your laptop in a daypack and hike to a favorite spot in a local park. I spent the last seven years of my agency career in a basement office with no window; perhaps you have a similar story of your own Cubicle, Sweet Cubicle or a white-walled, melamine-sheathed cell in your current job. Get out *now*.

5. **The savings bonanza.** What do you spend in an average year on dry cleaning? How often do you feel compelled to buy an all-new career wardrobe to keep up with the style choices of your colleagues? How much do you have to pay to park your car every day, or to commute by train or bus to work? What does your driving commute cost you in gas every week? Add all of these expenses up, and then delete them from your budget. I'm not saying that you will never have to buy another new suit, but working from home dramatically diminishes the need to buy five new suits every season. The more business is done by phone and e-mail, the less often you will need to see your clients in person—and with no office to travel to every day, you soon will find yourself working in jeans and a T-shirt and accomplishing just as much as you did in your corporate job, or even more. And forget about those commuting, parking, and gas expenses. Eliminating those will feel like you just got a big raise.

The Five Biggest Work-at-Home Pitfalls

I've painted a rosy picture of the work-at-home life, and indeed, it can be a true pleasure after decades of work for others. There are equal and opposite reactions, however, that can limit your sense of freedom and challenge your ability to compartmentalize work and home as separate entities.

1. **Your parents think you've retired.** Generally, our parents can't figure out what we do for a living anyway: "So, you didn't write the story, and you didn't do what's in the story, so what did you do?" Now that you're doing it from home, it's entirely likely that your relatives won't understand at all that you are legitimately working and running a business from your home office or living room. You can reiterate on a daily basis, and your mother will still call at 2:00 in the afternoon and wonder why you're not watching television or

doing laundry. It's a nagging frustration, but it's a small one in the grand scheme of distractions.

2. **The ever-present desk.** When you start your home-based business, you will need to work hard—and one of your toughest tasks will be to establish a time when you will push back from your desk and rejoin the world of the living. With your work right there in the building with you twenty-four hours a day, seven days a week, you will feel tempted to work during every waking moment. We'll talk in chapter 3 about strategies to separate yourself from the ever-present workload looming in the next room, but for the moment, let me say that you must create that separation and stick to it if your home-based business is to succeed. Otherwise, you will find yourself at odds with your spouse or partner, your children, and even with your own happiness. No one likes an obsessive workaholic, especially you.

3. **The dishes have voices.** What's more important: doing the breakfast dishes, or finishing that presentation? Generally, the presentation takes precedence, because you earn money while doing it . . . but the dishes seem to grow vocal cords and call to you like sirens calling Ulysses. Dishes, laundry, picking up after the kids, and home renovation or repair projects can become major distractions to productivity during your workday, no matter what your gender or your household role may be. It's imperative that you think of these tasks the way you would if you were still working for someone else's company: The dishes or laundry will wait until after work, just as they would if you were not in the house all day. (Meanwhile, there's no rule against folding the laundry or vacuuming the kids' rooms on a lunch break, if your time permits.)

4. **Boundaries . . . or barricades?** When the kids come home from school or your spouse returns from work, the tug-of-war begins: You're still working, but they want your time and attention. You may even have planned that working from home would allow you to spend more time with your children, especially if you are their transportation to extracurricular activities or you want to attend as many of their events as you can. If your new business provides primary financial support for your family, however, you and your family need to take your work hours seriously. Establishing boundaries from your first day can be a tricky business, but it must be done—and teaching your family to stick to these boundaries may require some toughness on

your part. Eventually, the new rules will become habit, and you will have better luck with conducting interviews, writing, and doing account work even with the television blaring in the next room. We'll talk about strategies for work-family separation in chapter 3.

5. **The world's longest job description.** During Minetor & Company's first weeks, I thought I would miss my friends from the agency, and the camaraderie we shared while brainstorming creative solutions. In reality, I missed only one

Thinkpoint: The Deathbed Test

If you're still wondering if forming your own home-based PR business is right for you, here's a question that can help clarify the future for you. I call this the Deathbed Test, and I still use this regularly to determine whether I'm heading down the right path.

On the last day of your life, when you're lying on your deathbed, what will you wish you'd done?

- Will you wish you'd made more money to put in your employer's pockets?

- Will you wish you'd spent more time in a beige cubicle?

- Will you wish you'd fought more traffic and made it to more meetings?

- Or will you wish you'd taken the risk and really tested your own mettle, and reaped the rewards that come with personal success?

- Will you wish you'd seen more of your family and been part of more of their activities?

- Will you wish you'd had the option of choosing your own clients and working with people whose goals and causes you were proud to support?

The questions you ask yourself may be completely different, but the results tend to be the same. We believe that we work for the paycheck and the juicy benefits, but when the day comes to assess our life's accomplishments, we see the world from a different perspective. Rarely do we wish we'd spent more time at someone else's office.

person from that office: Bill Hardy, the courier who picked up and delivered work materials to and from our clients and vendors. Suddenly without a support staff, I found myself doing tasks I hadn't done since my summers as an office temp—stuffing envelopes, running out to make pickups at client sites, rushing to Kinko's to make twenty copies of a document before a meeting. Super-fast Internet connectivity and file transfer protocol (FTP) have eliminated the need for many of these activities, but the fact remains that when you work from home, you are your own support staff. Collating documents, maintaining files, troubleshooting your computer issues, replacing the ink in your printer, and cleaning the bathroom are all in your new job description. The upside of all this, of course, is that you become more resourceful and self-sufficient than you ever imagined.

Your Business, Your Way

Putting the letters "CEO" after your name on your own business card packs a sweet head rush, but with it comes a sudden and staggering sense of responsibility. You've just become the head of strategy, sales, copywriting, creative, media contact, production, and accounting, all with a few dots of ink from your printer.

It's time to get busy bringing in clients, and quickly. Let's talk about some approaches that work.

Generalization versus Specialization

Among the many decisions you will make about your new company is this: What kind of PR practitioner do you want to be? Choosing a focus—or making a conscious choice *not* to focus—will help you define the kinds of clients you want to pursue first.

Generalization

Many PR firms of every size choose to be **generalists.** These firms understand that whatever industries in which their clients happen to be, the basic tenets of sound communications strategies still prevail. Every client needs to tout its own products or services to the community it serves, whether these clients are multinational corporations, smaller manufacturing companies, service industry professionals firms, retailers, charities, or other kinds of nonprofit organizations. Having a strong PR skill set will allow these firms to aid any client that comes their way.

Being a public relations generalist carries some significant advantages. Chances are good that you will manage a diverse client base, a real plus for those of us who are easily bored by routine. You will develop knowledge about many different kinds of businesses and industries, giving you the breadth you need to prove your capabilities to potential clients. If you've come from an inside job with a corporation or nonprofit organization and you have tremendous depth in one field's issues and media, becoming a generalist can help you broaden your scope, opening you up to growth in a wide variety of directions.

When you're starting out in business for yourself, you may default automatically to the generalist position for one very good reason: It's possible that being too choosy about your clients will prevent you from creating the revenue stream you need to pay yourself regularly and cover your expenses. Let's not mince words: You've given up your steady paycheck and you need to make a living. It makes practical sense to approach any and all potential clients, and to seek every opportunity to build your book of business.

Specialization

Before you decide absolutely that your business will provide general public relations services, however, let's take a look at the advantages of **specialization.**

Whether you've been in PR for many years or you're a year out of college, chances are you've already worked with a fairly diverse group of clients and/or employers. Maybe you've spent the last ten years in the public relations department of a major manufacturing company in the photographic or office products sector, for example, or your career spans several agency positions in which you've served a wide range of local and regional clients in law, medicine, politics, or industry.

If you're a recent college graduate, you've probably come to PR by way of your experience with one or more internships—and you've held several summer and campus jobs to help pay for your education. Something drew you to public relations in the first place: maybe an interest in sports marketing, a love of the arts, or an ability to translate technological concepts into clear language.

If you're a journalist, chances are good that you have an established area of expertise in one or several topics: finance, technology, commerce, fashion, the arts, entertainment, religion, medicine, or one of hundreds of other areas. Perhaps you come from the trade side, where you've written about a specific vertical market for a number of years. You are already a specialist, and you have the clips to prove it. It makes solid, logical sense to pursue clients in your field who have seen your name and know your work, even if you've never met them before this.

Use the worksheet on page 17 to list every kind of experience you've had to date. You may see a pattern emerging, a depth of expertise that you didn't even realize you had.

1. Make two columns on a sheet of paper: CLIENT and INDUSTRY.
2. In the first column, list your current employer and all of your past employers. If you work for a public relations agency, list all of the clients for whom you've provided services.
3. In the second column, after each employer or client, write the industry in which this company or organization does business. For example, Eastman Kodak Company and Xerox Corporation both do business in "imaging." If you've worked for a hospital and two dental firms, these all fall into "medicine."
4. Look for connections you may miss in the first pass. A manufacturer of extruded plastic products and a bottler of hair care products can be listed separately as "plastics" and "cosmetics," or they can come together under the more general heading, "manufacturing." A company that makes products for municipal water distribution can be listed as "water" or "utility," while a client in electrical power distribution can be "electricity" or "utility." These companies may face similar issues, or the qualities of their audiences may be very much alike.
5. Using a highlighting marker, highlight all of the clients or employers in one industry. Use a highlighter in a different color to mark all of the client or employers in a second industry. Keep going until you run out of industries.

Do you see a pattern? You may never have made the connection between clients or employers before, but you may have built up a strong base of knowledge in dealing with a specific kind of client. This is a good place to start as you begin prospecting for your company's first customers.

CLIENT	INDUSTRY

Specialization offers a number of benefits that will help you grow your business. You will get to know the trade editors and writers in your market niche to a degree that is not always possible when you're working across many different industries. The rapport you build with these important contacts will help you place more stories in the top magazines and on the most visited websites in that field, which in turn builds your reputation as a savvy public relations professional.

Now, here's the most important question: What kind of client makes you excited to get up and get to your desk every morning? You may have considerable knowledge of an industry or a kind of business that could be very lucrative, but the idea of continuing to work in that sector may simply bore you to tears. This is not only a valid way of looking at your potential client base, it's highly relevant to the success of your business. If you have lots of work to do for a client but you find yourself clicking on your Angry Birds app every time you sit down to work on that business, your days will drag and you will resent the need to keep this client just for the receivables. That's not why you went into business for yourself, and it's not a recipe for success.

From the Field

Amy Blum Public Relations
(www.linkedin.com/pub/amy-blum/9/809/372)

"It's not about me, it's about the client. I should be invisible."

Twenty-six years ago, Amy Blum took maternity leave from her job as a music therapist, unsure whether she would return to work several months later.

In the interim, her husband—classical double-bassist James VanDemark—suggested she try her hand at managing his career as a recitalist, chamber musician, and guest orchestral soloist. With a sleeping baby near at hand, Blum began booking concerts for James, and preheating the media by contacting classical music stations and music writers at newspapers wherever he was performing. When the clippings began to pour in, she suddenly realized she had discovered a new, far more interesting career.

"I have a degree in music, so I didn't have to learn about the subject in order to have music clients," she said. "When James was off playing concerts in various cities, I would call the media in advance. He plays an unusual solo instrument, so they quickly realized there would be high reader interest in a story. I got a lot of traction, a lot of articles, stories, features, and radio interviews. I was really enjoying this way more than I was enjoying booking the concerts."

By the time their daughter was 15 months old, Blum had opened her own firm, and business was in full swing. "I was making contacts everywhere—and that was back when you had to pick up the phone and talk to a reporter," she said. "All of my contacts were more national than local, and that quickly translated into legitimacy."

Blum's office consisted of a typewriter, a desk, a chair, a performing arts resource directory, and a phone in a second-floor bedroom. "It was away from the hub of the house, and it had a door that closed," she said. "A neighborhood teenager looked after my daughter. I remember hearing her crying for me with the sitter. You have to figure out how you're going to handle that. . . . Because the sitter was young, I'd go and check in. But when you're on the phone with a client or a writer, you can't always do that. I remember vividly that when I was working, I was thinking about my daughter, and when I was with my daughter, I was thinking about work."

Blum's family grew, and she found part-time, home-based neighborhood day care for her younger daughter while the older one was at school. Her client roster grew as well, as word spread through the classical music industry that a savvy, music-knowledgeable PR person could represent solo musicians with great results. "You can't underestimate the value of being able to discuss with your clients what they do," she said. "And I could pitch to the media in a comfortable way; I sounded like an expert. If I didn't know how to speak music, these music writers would know."

Soon Amy numbered among her clients a well-known classical record label, international media relations for the prestigious Eastman School of Music at the University of Rochester, and local and national PR for a major nonprofit orchestra, a gig that became a near full-time job for several years.

"People suggested that I should have submitted all that national and international press for awards," she said, "but it's not about me, it's about the client. I should be invisible. The best PR is about the client. If your ego makes you uncomfortable with that, you should think twice about being in PR."

Today Blum works from her first-floor home office in a larger house, where she has enough room and resources to bring in interns from the Eastman School and teach them her craft. She's traded the typewriter for a desktop computer, and she splits her time between her music clients and a new position: director of marketing and PR for Ganondagan State Historic Site, for which she also works from home.

While she uses all the digital conveniences that have become tools of the PR trade, Blum continues to believe in an aspect of the old-fashioned approach. "It's fine to have an e-mail relationship, but I still ask for a couple of minutes to chat by phone when I first contact someone new," she said. "It sounds old school, but it's really important. It's harder to be ignored when you've had a voice conversation with the recipient of your pitch. And you must think like a reporter. It's not what you think they should be interested in, it's what they do take an interest in. With the right knowledge and information, they can shift their perception and see the news value in your story."

Old school, maybe . . . but after twenty-six years as a home-based PR business owner, Blum knows what works.

Choosing a Business Name

Oh, the agonizing choice of the right name for your business! Should you be cute and catchy? Will it appear arrogant to use your own name? Should you make up a whole new word? What does your business name reveal about you and your new company?

You can brainstorm for weeks and come up with all kinds of names, but it may be faster and more effective to cut to the chase and take a simpler approach. Here are some name-finding strategies with proven track records.

1. If you have a strong, positive, personal reputation that makes your name an asset to your company, then it's common sense to use your own name as your company name. If you've worked in your field for a number of years, potential

clients will Google your name when they hear through the grapevine that you've started your own business. You can make yourself easy to find by naming the company after yourself (as I did with Minetor & Company).

2. Your own name can become a springboard for a more descriptive company moniker. "Maggie Jones Public Relations" is a name that makes the company's purpose and activity clear. It's clean, simple, and to the point.

3. If you are fairly new to the PR business and you don't have an established reputation, you may want to consider going for an evocative name that tells potential clients something about your company. For example, when Mallory Blair and Bianca Caampued went into business together in their early twenties, they were relative unknowns in the New York City retail PR scene. Just about five feet tall each, they chose a solid name for their new enterprise: Small Girls Big Business. Today Small Girls PR is one of the hottest PR microfirms in the city—not because of their name, but because of the energy with which they have imbued their identity, through their skills in social networking, event production, and working the media on their clients' behalf.

4. Cuteness can go terribly wrong, however. Today we must consider not only how our name will look on our business cards, but also how it will work as a domain name. Certainly the owners of the customized pen manufacturer Pen Island would have reconsidered if they realized that their name would appear as penisland.com. The people who founded Who Represents, a website on which you can find the agent for any famous actor, clearly did not think things through before they purchased the domain name whorepresents.com.

5. Avoid names that are so odd, out of context, or convoluted that they obscure your company's purpose. Such names are often the result of bringing together two words to make one new one, thus obscuring the meaning of either. Others sound like you've spent weeks pawing through a thesaurus to find the most esoteric word for your services, perhaps choosing a word so ambiguous that your clients will think they're not smart enough to work with you. You might just as well name your firm Incomprehensible Communications or Puffery PR if you go too far off the deep end in your naming strategy.

6. If you have a long list of possible names and you're struggling to choose one, use a search engine to help you narrow down your options. Business names become legal trademarks simply because a business is operating using that name, so you want to be sure that the name you choose is available, and that

it won't conflict with another company's name or imply that you are associated with another company. Be careful not to fall in love with a particular business name before you've made sure that an existing company in PR or a similar field has not already made your perfect name its own.

In chapter 5, we'll talk about the simple steps involved in securing your company name through a "doing business as" (DBA) registration.

B2B or B2C . . . or Both?

Hand in hand with the generalist versus specialist decision comes another focus: Do you prefer working in the business-to-business (B2B) world, or the wider field of business-to-consumer (B2C)?

In B2C public relations, you will work to reach consumers—usually in a specific demographic, but in a wide market—with messages about retail products and services or opportunities to connect with nonprofit organizations through donations, volunteerism, or use of the services they provide. The B2C PR firm reaches wide and digs deep, looking for every possible avenue through which to reach the target audience. National campaigns for retail products often come with sizable budgets that make every PR professional salivate, but they also come with high expectations and the need to make significant investments in contact management software, media lists, and the time required to follow up with hundreds of editors and producers.

B2B public relations—also known as trade media relations—works in the market niches inhabited by companies that make products used by other companies. Inherently less glamorous than B2C PR, trade PR often requires an ability to understand technology or industrial processes that may not interest the average communications professional. If your eyes glaze over when you hear words like "extrusion" and "supply chain," this may not be the field for you. However, B2B PR can provide a cyclical, dependable revenue stream from year to year as your stable of manufacturing companies releases a standard number of new products annually, attends the same trade shows and conferences each year, and functions on a work cycle that allows you to plan around a predictable cash flow. Your trade media lists and contact schedule may be manageable in Outlook, Mac Mail, or another mail and contact program without a staggering outlay of funds for dedicated software.

You may prefer a blend of B2C and B2B clients to keep your receivables high and your account management skills sharp. The ultimate choice is yours, but keep in mind that new business prospects will look for similarities between the work you do now and the work they intend to offer you, so your early choices of accounts and specialties will have an impact on the work you can get down the road.

Expanding Your Skills

No matter what situation you're leaving as you start your own business, you cannot possibly know everything you need to know. You may be a whiz at pitching and winning new clients, but your accounting skills barely extend to balancing your personal checkbook. Or you're great at business processes and account management, but you've never had to sell your own services, and the idea of selling makes you shudder as if you've discovered a tarantula in your shoe.

When you run your own home-based business, your job description covers every possible position. It's time to be honest with yourself about what you know and what you don't, and to think about the ways you can gain the skills to fill the gaps in your repertoire.

Once you've developed a list of areas in which you will need extra help, there are plenty of ways to close the skill gaps.

1. **Take a course.** Your local community or business college almost certainly offers courses in bookkeeping for non-financial people, contact database management, and other nuts-and-bolts subjects that can help you pick up the business process skills you need. Night courses allow you to start building these skills even before you leave your current job. You probably won't need a master's degree in business administration to run your home-based PR business, so save this monumental commitment until you're seriously considering a major growth plan.

   College courses also can help if your PR skills are limited to a single client or industry, or to very specific situations. For example, if you've been the community PR representative of your local or state police force, you may have considerable depth in dealing with daily print, television, radio, and web reporters, but no experience at all in working with the lucrative field of retail product publicity. A college course from a respected university that offers a public relations major can help you apply your street-smart skills to the private sector. By

What You Do and Don't Know

Here is a list of many of the skills you're likely to need in your business. After each of these, check your response in the spaces provided: Can Do It Now, Can Learn to Do, or Don't Want to Do. For each task that you choose Don't Want to Do, fill in a potential supplier for this task.

	Can Do It Now	Can Learn to Do	Don't Want to Do
PR-Related Skills			
Account management	_____	_____	_____
General writing	_____	_____	_____
Editing	_____	_____	_____
Building media lists	_____	_____	_____
Media contact	_____	_____	_____
Contact management	_____	_____	_____
News release writing	_____	_____	_____
Feature writing	_____	_____	_____
Event planning	_____	_____	_____
Social media	_____	_____	_____
Writing PR plans	_____	_____	_____
Writing proposals	_____	_____	_____
Online research	_____	_____	_____
Blogging	_____	_____	_____
Website design	_____	_____	_____
Website content	_____	_____	_____
Facebook page building	_____	_____	_____
Graphic design	_____	_____	_____
Print production	_____	_____	_____
Video production	_____	_____	_____
Business Growth			
Networking	_____	_____	_____
Cold-calling	_____	_____	_____
Sales presentations	_____	_____	_____
RFP* responses	_____	_____	_____
Online research	_____	_____	_____
Lead generation	_____	_____	_____

* Request for Proposal (see chapter 6)

	Can Do It Now	Can Learn to Do	Don't Want to Do
Business Management			
Bookkeeping	_____	_____	_____
Tax preparation	_____	_____	_____
Payroll preparation	_____	_____	_____
Time management	_____	_____	_____
Writing contracts	_____	_____	_____
Legal issues	_____	_____	_____
Insurance issues	_____	_____	_____
IT maintenance	_____	_____	_____
IT troubleshooting	_____	_____	_____
Supervising staff	_____	_____	_____
Crisis management	_____	_____	_____
Cleaning	_____	_____	_____
Filing	_____	_____	_____
TOTAL	_____	_____	_____

Add up the number of checkmarks in each column. How many things do you need to learn to do? How many skills will you need to depend on outside sources to provide—and where will you go for these services?

While you can't know everything on your first day in business, putting together a plan to find and call on trusted suppliers will save you much time and aggravation later, when you're in a time crunch and you need services quickly.

the same token, if you're a corporate PR professional moving into politics or entertainment publicity, you may need some additional study to understand how your skills translate to your new field. If there's no nearby university, look for a mentor who's already doing the kind of PR you want to do. You may want to consider freelancing to this person for a reduced fee or even for free (for a limited time) while you observe and build your own skills.

2. **Attend professional seminars.** The Public Relations Society of America (PRSA) offers seminars in major cities across the country, as well as online webinars through which you can access the expertise of top PR profession-

als. Most of these learning experiences center on a specific skill area: strategic communications planning, media training, social media, technology, writing, measurement, and others. PRSA records some seminars and makes them available for playback on demand on the organization's website, www.prsa.org. Click on the "Learning" button and select "All Events" to see the full list of offerings.

3. **Hire it out.** There may be tasks that will be better provided by a trusted advisor or a crackerjack support person—things that are not a good use of your time. Few business owners should complete their own income tax returns, for example, because of the specialized expertise required. Or you may be a brilliant PR practitioner but a disaster at office organization and management, so a part-time assistant who can keep your databases up to date and your office pristine may be just what you need. If you can afford to engage the proper outside suppliers, they can be a worthwhile investment, as their services will save you the time and money you would spend learning to perform these tasks yourself.

4. **Get a tutor.** If your skill gap is software-based, you can find qualified people in your area who can help you learn to use an application that's new to you. For example, the bookkeeping software giant QuickBooks offers an online database that you can search by zip code to find a certified advisor in your area (visit http://proadvisor.intuit.com/fap/). Sage ACT!, one of the best-known contact management applications, also certifies its own advisors throughout the United States and its territories; you can find one in your area at http://sagesoftwarecertifiedconsultants.com.

5. **Teach yourself.** Thanks to the web, just about every hardware or software manufacturer has a knowledge base section of its website, stocked with constructive comments, hints, work-arounds, and lots of other advice from people who actually use their products. If your skill gap involves technology, you'll find a wealth of free advice online that can help you get past the Welcome page in any program you want to use. Searchable online manuals and Help buttons have replaced voluminous instruction books, making it easy to find answers to specific questions. If you are fairly facile with new apps, you can get up and running without a great deal of fuss.

From the Field

Sally Cohen, Sally Cohen PR

IS THERE LIFE AFTER TELEVISION NEWS?

When thirteen years as the arts and entertainment reporter for "R News" on a cable news channel in Rochester, New York, came to an abrupt end, Sally Cohen had to ask herself some hard questions.

"I'd been in the music and theater business for twenty-five years before R News," she said. Well-known in the area because of her popularity as the lead singer and songwriter for Backseat Sally, a hot regional rock 'n' roll group, Cohen had built a natural following that gave her an instant audience for her coverage of local theater, film, dance, music, and art exhibitions. One of her compelling stories even caught the attention of producers at CNN, and found its way onto the national news.

As beloved as she was by the arts community, however, Cohen and her features were cut from an ever-decreasing budget. "I was heartbroken," she said. "I tried to get back into TV, but I think that no one felt they could make a profit by covering the arts. So I went to a career counseling service, and they helped me narrow my focus. After six months, I decided what I wanted to do: I would be a publicist for the arts."

Was she nuts? Cohen understood the struggle she might have to make a living by working for some of the area's most underfinanced individuals and organizations, but she swallowed her fears and moved forward. "I hung out my shingle on my own, and I have never been without work since," she said.

She signed on to work on the PR staff of the Rochester International Jazz Festival, and learned the trade from some of the most successful and respected arts promoters in upstate New York. She took on the promotion of an independent film being produced in the area, reintroducing herself to the local media in her new persona as publicist. She served as an interim public relations director for the Eastman School of Music, one of the most respected music schools in the world.

Now, years after leaving TV news, Cohen has built a stable clientele. "I don't worry about it anymore," she said. "It just happens. The Arts & Cultural Council of Greater Rochester recommends me, and satisfied clients recommend me, and I keep getting referrals."

With an innate understanding of the artist's mindset, temperament, and personal and monetary challenges, Cohen developed a rapport with all kinds of artists. "I can make money, because I have no overhead," she said, "but I find that I discount my hours, because I know what they can afford. And I put a lot of passion into my work—something I don't charge for. I'll work with them to get their goals accomplished."

Her greatest triumph came when an Associated Press stringer did a story with photos about artist Larry Moss and his specialized art form, which he calls "Airigami"—a combination of sculpting and puppetry, executed entirely with balloons. When Moss created a ten-room, 10,000-square-foot haunted house made with 100,000 balloons, AP sent the story nationwide. "When we woke up the next day, it was on newspapers and websites all over the world—thousands and thousands of them," Cohen said. "CNN Headline News picked it up, and later Larry was on the *Today Show* and the *Martha Stewart Show*. What a thrill! Until then, when I said that I handled a balloon artist, it made me sound like Broadway Danny Rose. But now, Larry is by far my most recognized client."

Cohen put Airigami on the map, and Airigami lifted Sally Cohen PR to a new, lofty height. She branched out beyond the arts and took on clients including an architectural firm and an engineering firm, and she continues to enjoy a steady stream of referrals. She handles all of this from a tiny office in her home in Fairport, a suburb of Rochester, where she looks out on a forever-wild landscape of coniferous trees beyond her backyard.

At first, she shared this compact space with her self-employed husband, David, a musician who is often off-site teaching or recording. As Sally's business grew, he moved his work into another room. Their daughter, Sammi, graduated from college in 2011, but for several years, Sally split her time between her home-based business and her daughter's schedule. "I never felt I could go back into the music business after Sammi was born," she said. "My passion for music translated into my passion for her. It was nice to be home when she was in high school—I started working in television when she was three. That was hard, so it was better to be at home and accessible."

Even with her flexible schedule and her highly visible successes, Cohen faces some crazy days with her unusual clients. "It bothers me when I build a relationship with someone, and they shut me down," she said. "When they can't afford it or they don't quite trust that I know what I'm doing, we end up not doing as good a job as we could have. But when they take my advice and run with it, it works. That's the best."

APR Certification: Do You Need It?

The only official professional certification for PR people is PRSA's Accredited in Public Relations (APR) credential. PRSA established this rigorous testing standard in 1964, and to date, the organization's website says that more than five thousand people have passed the exam and received the accreditation. The Bureau of Labor Statistics tells us that in 2008, 275,200 people held jobs in public relations, so fewer than 1 percent of all of these PR professionals have chosen to take the exam (which in 2011 carried a hefty $410 price tag) and add this credential to their business cards.

The accreditation, according to PRSA's website, "measures a public relations practitioner's fundamental knowledge of communications theory and its application; establishes advanced capabilities in research, strategic planning, implementation and evaluation, and demonstrates a commitment to professional excellence and ethical conduct." APR-credentialed PR professionals are required to continue their professional education through courses, volunteer work, or other activities that keep them up to date with current trends, tools, and other aspects of the public relations industry.

Perhaps most important in today's media world, in which PR people have been painted as spin doctors who convolute messages to avoid disclosing facts, the APR credential legitimizes our profession and demonstrates that we are held to a high standard. Its emphasis on communications theory and planning, as well as on professional ethics, makes the APR a strong endorsement of an individual's commitment to sound business practices.

These are all worthwhile reasons to consider APR, but how they apply to your home-based PR business will depend entirely on the kind of PR you want to practice, and the clients you hope to attract.

Here's the bottom line: If you pitch a client who has an APR after her name, you will have a much better chance of winning the account if you have the APR credential as well. If most of your clients hire you because they have no PR skills and they need you to be their adjunct public relations department, the accreditation may be less important, as these clients probably have never heard of APR.

The Tough Transition: Leaving Your Full-Time Job

So the day has come, and you're ready to make the leap from your full-time position to business ownership. Congratulations! Here are some important guidelines to help you make this transition in the most honorable, least controversial, and smoothest way possible.

Should You Freelance While You're Still Employed?

Whether you work in a PR agency or you have a corporate, private, or nonprofit position, most employers frown on their employees taking on freelance work, even when it will not conflict directly with the work you do on the job.

There are some good, sound reasons for this. Freelance work inevitably bleeds into the workday, as you get calls from your freelance clients in the middle of meetings, use your lunch breaks to meet with outside folks or to do phone interviews, or actually do the freelance work during your time at the office. None of these activities sit well with the employer who is paying you to do his work during certain hours.

If you're in an agency position, freelance work creates an uncomfortable conflict of interest. It's understood that agency employees will bring all work opportunities into the agency, rather than completing them on their own time. Even if you have never signed a non-competition agreement (more on this in a moment), doing business with companies that could and should be agency clients will not go well for you, especially if you attempt to hide this from your employer. Some agency owners would even consider this grounds for termination.

When agencies are highly specialized, however, it may be acceptable to your employer if you take on some limited projects that the agency would never consider as viable clients. Charitable organizations, nonprofits with whom you have a pre-existing personal relationship, or small companies that could never afford your agency's services may all be freelance opportunities that will not conflict with your agency's direction and goals. If you choose to pursue this kind of work, be up front with your employer about what you're doing. You are entitled to have personal interests, and your employer may even admire your willingness to help worthwhile causes with limited budgets.

How to Break Up

No one walks away from a job situation that's been totally fulfilling and delightful every day, so it's entirely likely that you're looking at this significant change because you're not especially happy where you are.

This may be no secret to your employer. No matter how stoically you believe you've suffered, most managers know when they've got an unhappy employee on their hands. With this in mind, before you walk into your boss's office and flatly tender your resignation, it's a good time to assess your relationship and determine the best way to announce your intention to open your own firm.

If you're in a corporate or nonprofit job, you're on excellent terms with your management, and you feel comfortable doing so, you can consider discussing your goal with your current employer. This will allow you to set an end date that works for you and your manager, with an interim during which you can train others to cover your job responsibilities, write up descriptions of processes you use in your job, and wind down in a manner that reduces the stress of losing a prized employee. Your employer will appreciate the time, and you can have an amicable separation at the end of the severance period. Some corporations permit ex-employees to contract back to the company after a set interval, so you may even preserve a relationship that will turn into a client.

If you work for a public relations firm or advertising agency, however, the announcement that you intend to start your own firm will not be met quite as pleasantly. It's a fact of life that you have been servicing clients for this agency, and that some, if not all, of your clients have benefitted from your services—and they expect to work with you again. This makes you a competitor with the agency, and no matter how beloved you were during your tenure, your announcement that you are starting your own firm makes you an instant outsider. Don't bother being offended by the sudden change in your employer's attitude; it's a situation of your own design, and it's part of the business. Your management may be willing to have you remain for a few days to clean up loose ends, but your employer will want you out of there as quickly and cleanly as possible.

If you do stay for a severance period, be prepared to face locked filing cabinets that used to be open to everyone, sudden changes in everyone's network passwords, and locks changed on the outer doors—especially if you were a principal in the firm. This does not mean that they no longer like you, or that they truly feel you are an enemy or a crook. Do not take any of this as a stab at your professional integrity—that way madness lies. Instead, accept it as a fact of business ownership. Indeed, it's a sort of compliment: Your employer respects your skills, and believes that you will present a real competitive liability once you're in the field. (Your employer is right. You know all of his weaknesses, so you know how to sell against him if you choose to do so.)

Rather than going to all this trouble, the management may simply accept your resignation, allow you to clean out your desk, and then walk you to the door. This can happen in any kind of business, sometimes without precedent or warning. It's tough to prepare yourself emotionally to sever ties this quickly, but the good news is that you won't need to hang around for days writing descriptions of job processes, training your interim replacement, or having long exit interviews. You can get on with the next chapter in your career, and it's a darned exciting one. Accept this gift of time, get out, and get going.

Honoring Non-Competition Agreements

If you worked for a public relations firm or advertising agency, you may have been required to sign a **non-competition agreement** as a condition of your employment. This agreement may restrict you from approaching any existing clients of the firm for a set period of time—usually a year—after you leave the agency. Some such agreements actually restrict you from pursuing the same profession in competition with this employer. Your agency's management required this because they were afraid that you would do exactly what you are about to do: start a competitive business, using skills you honed while in their employ, and making the most of trade secrets and inside information you gained as an employee of this firm.

Before you laugh this off, consider the case of Chris Botticella, a senior vice president with Thomas' English Muffins. In 2010, Botticella decided it was time to move on in his career, so he took a presumably higher-paying position with Hostess, a significant competitor in the packaged baked goods industry. This kind of move happens all the time, but there was a catch: Botticella is one of only seven people in the entire world who know the secret recipe that gets those nooks and crannies into Thomas' English Muffins. When he announced his resignation, the Thomas' company waved the vice president's non-competition agreement at him and insisted that he could not take the job, because he held such a major trade secret. The case went to court . . . and Thomas' English Muffins won. Botticella had to pass on the Hostess job.

You may think, "I don't know any secret recipes," but you do. You know what business processes make your agency employer successful. You know what tricks you used to impress the prospects in your big presentations, and you know what internal systems your agency uses to generate new business or to produce high-quality work. Now you're going to start your own firm—and while you may be a sole proprietor today, your boss knows what a dynamo you are and what you can accomplish. Next thing you know, he's waving that non-compete agreement at you and threatening a court battle.

Non-compete agreements are notoriously hard to enforce, especially those that are written to keep you from working in PR anywhere at all, ever. Enforceable agreements establish a time period and a geographic area in which you cannot practice your trade, giving your former employer a cushion in which to reinforce her own standing with clients before you unleash your talents onto the world at large.

Whether or not your employer can enforce any kind of non-competition agreement also depends on where you live. California, for example, has been known to invalidate these agreements unless you actually own an equity share of the company you're leaving. Other states, including California, restrict such agreements to activity within the state in which they were written—so if you plan to relocate to start your business, you're out of the agreement's jurisdiction. Some states throw out any agreement that unreasonably restricts the ex-employee's ability to earn a living.

Wherever you live, however, you will need an attorney to go to bat for you if you want to begin building your new business while this agreement is in effect.

If you know that you signed a non-competition agreement, get your copy to an attorney *before* you resign from your job. If there's no way out of the contract, you may need to rethink your business plans between your last day at the agency and the last day that the agreement is in effect.

Beyond the specifics of the non-compete clause, there may be other restrictive covenants in the contract that can affect your ability to launch your new business. A **forfeiture-for-competition agreement,** for example, may require you to forfeit some benefits to engage in competitive activities. A **compensation-for-competition agreement** could require you to actually pay your former employer for doing business that could be classified as competitive. A **nonsolicitation agreement** prohibits you from soliciting any of your employer's clients—and some such agreements even prohibit you from taking business from these clients if they approach you of their own accord. Your attorney can help you sort through what may be enforceable in your state, and what clauses may actually cripple your ability to set up your own business.

You also may be bound indefinitely by a **nondisclosure agreement** or a **confidentiality agreement.** These are very common tools in the communications industry, often administered by the clients themselves. Nondisclosure is a promise not to share the client's or company's confidential information with anyone outside of the client company or your public relations firm. Generally, these won't keep you from doing business, as long as you work with the utmost integrity and keep mum about your former clients' confidential information, especially when you work for their competitors.

Your contract may also have a clause called "garden leave," which requires you to give at least ninety days' notice before leaving your job. No one wants to sit around being the lame duck at their job for ninety days, so after the usual two-week period (or less, as we've discussed), you're forced to sit at home and wait out the rest of the ninety days until you can work again. Meanwhile, your former employer is busy cementing relationships with the clients you might consider approaching for business.

If your attorney feels that the contract is enforceable, and if you're not willing to go through an expensive court battle to find out otherwise, you may need to cool your heels for a time while you wait out the term of the agreement. There's no way to start the clock on the non-compete restriction except to leave your job, so if you want to launch your own firm, you're going to need some other source of income during the year that the contract specifies.

Can You Take Clients with You?

If there's no non-competition agreement in place, you will be tempted to call on some of your former clients and sign them for your new venture.

Even without a contract expressly forbidding you to do so, however, you can still run up against some serious legal issues. In forty-three states, the Uniform Trade Secrets Act prohibits former employees from using their employers' client lists to build their new businesses. (Massachusetts, New Jersey, New York, Pennsylvania, Tennessee, Texas, and Wyoming have their own statutes that protect trade secrets.) The client list is considered a trade secret, a chunk of information not available to the general public. Even if you don't have a physical copy of the list and you're working from memory—specifically, from the memory of working with these clients yourself—the list is still a trade secret in the eyes of the law. You may protest that the agency posts a list of its clients on its website, a common defense in such cases, but the contact names at each company are considered proprietary. The Uniform Trade Secrets Act protects the employer for three years, so the resulting legal action could put your new venture out of business.

If you have no intention of approaching your employer's current clients—and at this point, you've seen that it's really unwise—make sure that you don't do anything that will trigger your employer's suspicion that you are getting ready to solicit these companies for business.

- Don't spend long periods at the copier, making copies of old files in front of whoever may pass by.
- Don't send yourself e-mails from your business computer to your home address with files and information attached.
- Don't spend an hour in the sample room gathering up examples of the work you've done for the last several years.
- Don't make calls or send e-mails from your office to old clients with whom you haven't worked in some time.
- Don't take time out of your agency workday to have coffee with former clients. This may be something you would do as a matter of course as an agency principal or account executive, but once you resign, such a get-together will look like a preemptive solicitation.

Contracting Back to Your Employer

In some cases, your employer may be eager to keep you and your skills in the fold, offering you contract work at your new hourly rate (see chapter 6) or a rate specified by the company's contracting policy.

Such an arrangement can create a dependable revenue stream while you build your new client base. While the work may be exactly what you did before—which may be just what you're hoping to escape—you will have the additional flexibility of working from home instead of in the office, which will help you ease into your new, independent life.

If you're hoping to establish this kind of relationship with your current employer, check into the company's rules for contracting former employees before you resign. This will give you an idea of what's possible, so you can offer your services to your current manager with all the information she needs to decide if she'd like to keep you on these new terms.

Contracting will not offer you the benefits you have as an employee, but it may give you enough of an income base to buy health insurance and continue your contributions to your retirement plan until you have enough new accounts to finance these requirements.

Your First Day of Freedom

You're out.

The safety net is gone and you're flying free, going where the next gust of wind takes you. It's your first day without the bonds of indentured servitude, and from now on, you're not just your own boss—you're the Chief Executive Officer. You make the decisions. You bring home the bacon. You're the master of your domain.

Sure, it's a little scary, but let's remember why you made this move. No more Cubicle Prison. No more offices without windows. No more working with clients you hate on accounts that bore you to tears. No more ducking your boss's mood swings, or drinking the terrible coffee the receptionist makes so you won't hurt her feelings. Right now, go get yourself your favorite fancy coffee shop drink and put your feet up. Savor the independence, and see what's going on in the world in the middle of the day. Take stock of where you've been, where you are today, and where you want to go next.

Wasn't that nice? Okay, break's over. Let's get to work.

03

Your Home-Based Corporate Headquarters

Setting up your home office can be almost as much fun as working in it. If your budget permits you some personal expression and creativity, there's no limit to the kind of environment you can create. Those cartoons your previous employer thought were "inappropriate"? Hang them on the wall! That fabulous, bright raspberry paint you've wished you had a room for? Surround yourself with it! You need to create an office where you look forward to spending your time . . . because believe me, you're going to spend a lot of time there.

The Space

Let's get down to the basics: the where, what, and why of your office space.

Your office needs to be a place where you can conduct business like the professional you are, whether or not you ever bring a client or supplier into this inner sanctum. You'll need to establish a level of decorum here, something that's not always easy when you're working from home. You need good lighting, relative quiet, and some separation from the chaos that most of us consider our non-working lives. Here are some office ground rules that will help you choose and equip your new corporate headquarters.

Where: Location, Location, Location!

Ideally, you need an office with a door. You will want the door for two reasons: (1) Sometimes you'll want to shut out your family's everyday tumult and commotion, and (2) Sometimes you'll want to shut the door with you on the outside, and take some time to be a family member again.

For most of us, it seems that every square inch of the house is already gainfully occupied. Take a good, honest look at your home, however, and you may be surprised at the space that's available to clean out and repurpose. Maybe there's a spare room filled with boxes of whatnot that you haven't opened since you moved in. Perhaps there's a playroom your kids used when they were smaller, and now it's chock-full of games and toys they once loved, but no longer need. There might be a guest room that rarely actually sees guests. There's a corner of the basement that doesn't need to be loaded with Lucite punch bowls, Christmas reindeer that no longer glimmer, and braided leather peace symbol necklaces from a decade you've all but forgotten. Somewhere in your home, there's a room you can turn into a profit center—the most persuasive argument ever for cleaning it out.

Be honest with yourself about the space you've found. My first home office—very briefly—was in the attic of our house, where it was about 120 degrees on a summer day. I actually sat and wrote my first proposals up there while we renovated our tiny spare room, and after two weeks beneath the rafters, I thought the sixty-three air-conditioned square feet into which I moved was the world's most comfortable office.

You deserve to work comfortably, especially if your new business will make a significant contribution to your household income. Use the screening list below to help you consider (and perhaps reconsider) the space you've carved out for your moneymaking enterprise.

A Room with a Window

A colleague of mine struggled with seasonal affective disorder (SAD), an all-too-frequent malady borne by those of us who live in the frigid North Country, where daylight wanes within eight hours from November to January. She noted that she worked in a "garden level" office in an advertising agency—a disturbing euphemism for an office in a basement. She arrived while murky dawn had barely broken, worked under artificial light all day, and left for home after sunset. For two or three months of every year, except for the occasional meeting, she only saw daylight on weekends. The result was a mind-numbing depression that severely limited her productivity and deadened her usually cheery disposition. Worse, the lack of daylight affected her circadian system, disrupting her sleep cycle with bouts of insomnia. We may be quick to recommend bright, all-spectrum light fixtures and regular "daylight breaks" for this coworker, but the real fact is this: No one should be forced to work in this kind of situation.

Most of us are not imprisoned in basements throughout the workday, but we may come from the world of Dilbert-style mazes with high walls that block whatever light comes from distant windows in the outer wall. These cubicle networks tend to

Home Office Location Screening Checklist

Environment questions:

- Is there natural light in this space during the day?

- Can I add enough light to see comfortably on darker days and at night?

- Can I get enough ventilation and regulate the temperature adequately during any season?

- Is there enough room for my desk, filing cabinets, sample storage, reference books, and other materials?

- How does this space smell? If it's musty or otherwise unpleasant, can it be fixed?

- Can I see clients in this space? If not, is there somewhere else in the house where I can meet with clients comfortably?

- Can I create a professional-looking background in this space for videoconferencing and meetings by Skype?

- Is there a door I can close when necessary? If not, is there another way to screen out household noise?

Power/connectivity questions:

- Are there enough electrical outlets? If not, how can I bring more into the space?

- Does my mobile phone get signal in this space?

- Can I get Wi-Fi or a hard line Internet connection here?

- Is there room for all of my peripherals—scanner, printer, and others?

be lit by buzzing fluorescent tubes overhead, sometimes supplemented with task lighting just above the work surface. Wouldn't it be great if you did not imitate this artificial environment in your own home?

In a study titled, "The Benefits of Daylight through Windows," conducted at the Lighting Research Center at Rensselaer Polytechnic Institute, researchers took on the task of quantifying the benefits of natural light in workplace situations. They determined that daylight has a greater probability of maximizing visual performance than most forms of electric light, "because it tends to be delivered in large amounts with a spectrum that ensures excellent color rendering." Beyond this practical consideration, the study concluded that, "Physiologically, daylight is an effective stimulant to the human visual system and the human circadian system," and "psychologically, daylight and a view are much desired." The study goes on to conclude, "Windows that provide a view out as well as daylight, can reduce stress and hence reduce the demand for health services. Daylight reduces the incidence of health problems caused by the rapid fluctuations in light output typical of electric lighting."

In short, you'll be happier in your home office if it has a window.

Your Desk

Your work surface can be whatever you wish: a favorite uncle's polished mahogany table, a modern mission-style executive desk of engineered wood, an IKEA some-assembly-required instant office kit, a hollow-core door you picked up at Mister Seconds and laid across a couple of two-drawer filing cabinets, or a Formica countertop with legs you built yourself.

The surface and construction don't matter nearly as much as the desk's overall functionality. You'll need space to work, whether you've got Apple's biggest tower computer or Dell's smallest laptop. Much as we would like to believe that we've entered the paperless era, your clients may not have made the leap just yet. Expect to acquire piles of reference materials from clients, papers and volumes that you will need to spread out on some kind of surface. You'll need places to keep notepads and pens; scissors; a stapler; envelopes for sending out invoices; printer paper; a manila folder for each project in progress; receipts; transaction records; a dictionary, thesaurus, and style manual; paper clips; rubber bands; and any number of other useful items.

So beyond the desk's surface, choose a hutch, shelves, sets of rolling wire baskets, drawer units, whatever will fit comfortably into your office and keep you relatively organized. Remember that the only way your office will be neat and well ordered is if you clean it up, so establish a system early on to contain the inevitable flotsam that every office accumulates.

Your Chair: Spare No Expense

There's one item in your office that you should never buy on the cheap: your chair.

You're going to sit in your chair for hours at a stretch, day after day, year after year. Do not grab the spare chair from your kitchen or dining room set, the metal folding chair you schlep out of the basement for Thanksgiving, or a molded plastic stack chair meant for your patio. This so-called furniture may be handy at no up-front cost, but the long-term damage to your back, neck, arms, and wrists will make you wish you'd spent some money up front for something that's actually made to support your body in comfort.

A good desk chair may cost you more than your computer, but it's an investment that will help keep you off of the physical therapist's table. Look for an ergonomic chair that can be adjusted to fit your own body, from the seat height and placement of your feet all the way to the arm rests. A chair made of mesh fabric will keep you cooler than a leather, fabric, or solid vinyl model, and adjustable lumbar support will take pressure off of your back during long writing sessions. While you may not want to spring for the name-brand chair that has become the standard in executive suites, many of the same features are available in slightly less luxuriously engineered knock-offs.

Your Office Machine Suite

Do you need a desktop tower computer, a laptop, or a tablet? To help you make the decision, the chart on pages 42–43 looks at all three. You may find that some combination will work best for you, especially if you plan to work from your favorite diner, library, coffee shop, or local park on a regular basis.

If your business is going to offer video production services for video news releases, event documentation, YouTube postings, and other applications, the higher processing speeds and performance of a desktop computer will be your first priorities. PR businesses that offer photographic services also may need more power, especially if you plan to spend time editing and improving photos in Photoshop, LightRoom, Aperture, or another photo production application. These highly visual tasks are best performed using one or more large monitors, making an even stronger case for a desktop tower computer as one of your key electronic tools.

If you believe that most of your time will be spent on writing, corresponding with editors and producers, and social networking on behalf of your clients, a laptop offers you the power and capabilities you need, with the added advantage of portability. Many laptops also have the processing power to handle video and photo editing, and some are even equipped with built-in cameras to allow videoconferencing and Skype calls with clients and editors at a distance. When you're in your home office, you can plug a larger monitor into a laptop to give you the visual capability you need for photo retouching and tricky video editing jobs.

A tablet computer will take your coolness factor to the max with clients, vendors, current and former colleagues, your teenage kids, and strangers who see you working at a cafe table in the local sandwich shop. It's a great accessory to your total computer ensemble, and it provides an effective tool for making presentations—just flip through your text, graphics, and photos on the tablet screen—and for taking notes in client and vendor meetings. If you've been writing since you were four, you may find typing on an on-screen keyboard to be a difficult, if not insurmountable, adjustment. (You can buy a tablet-compatible keyboard to carry with you, although this defeats some of the purpose of the sleek, self-contained tablet.) You may also find the available apps for business writing, spreadsheets, and presentation building to be less than adequate, both in their functionality and in their compatibility with your clients' documents and computer systems.

Thinkpoint: Which Platform?

Apple or PC? It hardly matters anymore, as the compatibility issues that once plagued both platforms have been largely eradicated. Your software choices are far more important, however, as your clients expect you to conform to their computer requirements. If they all work in Microsoft Word, for example, they will resist receiving documents created in Pages or Google Docs. You may be light years ahead of your clients in your technological savvy, but they won't be impressed if they feel you can't communicate in the manner they prefer.

	Desktop tower	Laptop	Tablet
Performance	Nearly always the most powerful, with the fastest processing speeds	Processing speed and memory capacity can rival desktop models in top-of-the-line laptops	Processing speed is as fast as or faster than laptop
Storage	Virtually unlimited: most start at 64–320GB or higher; upgrade to as much as 8 terabytes (TB)	Most start at 40–320GB, with limited ability to add storage	Recent models top out at 16, 32, or 64GB
Connectivity	Can use a wired or wireless Internet connection	Can use a wired, wireless, or Bluetooth Internet connection	Can use a Wi-Fi, Bluetooth, 3G, or 4G wireless connection
Monitor/screen	Separate monitor required, but any size is compatible	Built-in screen up to 17 inches; add a big external monitor for office use if desired	Bright touch-screen up to 9.7 inches

	Desktop tower	Laptop	Tablet
Portability	Stays put in your office	Goes anywhere, weighs about 3–5 pounds	Goes anywhere; about a third of a laptop's weight
Power	Always requires electrical connection	Up to 6 hours on battery life on a single charge, depending on the model. Can also run on electrical power.	Up to 10 hours of battery life on a charge
Interface	Mouse, trackball, or track pad as preferred	Most come with built-in track pad. Add a USB or wireless mouse or a USB trackball if preferred.	Touch screen. Tablet-compatible keyboards are available. Touch-screen keyboard may not be comfortable for typists accustomed to a conventional keyboard.
Peripherals (printer, scanner, DVD drive, etc.)	Compatible with all computer peripherals. Wi-Fi and Bluetooth cards required for wireless connections.	Compatible with all computer peripherals via USB or FireWire, Wi-Fi or Bluetooth (depending on model)	Connects to Wi-Fi or Bluetooth-enabled peripherals
Space requirement	Always lives on or under your desk; can require 9 cubic feet of space	Small footprint on your desk, no additional space underneath required	Notebook-sized footprint
Capabilities	Can run any software compatible with its operating system. Often the fastest for editing photos and video.	Can run any software compatible with its operating system. Top model with fastest processors can match desktop computers for speed in video and photo editing.	Can run tablet-compatible apps only, which precludes many business programs. Apple models are incompatible with Flash.
Susceptibility to damage/theft	Difficult to damage significantly; unlikely to get lost or stolen from your office unless you have a major break-in	Higher potential for damage from falling, beverage spills, etc. Can be left behind or stolen in public places.	Higher potential for loss or theft than desktop
Future-proof	Easy to upgrade with more processing power, additional memory	Difficult and costly to upgrade for greater processing power. Storage upgrades are easy.	Hardware and OS upgrades not currently possible

Printer

The paperless office is on its way, but it hasn't arrived quite yet. The good news is that the days of the printed press kit are definitely over. No one wants to mess with that much paper, least of all the media—many of whom will copy passages of your releases right into their stories (and isn't that the point of a good press kit?). So you may not need a production-quality laser printer with its oh-so-expensive toner cartridges.

Choosing a printer begins with its compatibility with your computer—you'll find that information printed in the "systems requirements" on the box as well as on the manufacturer's website. From there, you have many choices in terms of print quality, the number of functions beyond basic printing, and the cost of ink or toner.

Profit Booster

Do the math when you're buying a printer: The real investment is in ink, not in the printer itself. You can get an inkjet printer that provides excellent output for under $50 at your favorite discount warehouse, but every time you need ink, you're looking at more than $50 to purchase a black cartridge and an all-in-one color cartridge (or, worse, a separate one for each color). Think seriously about just buying a new printer when the ink runs out—it's actually cheaper in the long run, and you'll always have an up-to-date model.

All-in-one (AIO) units provide a printer, copier, and flatbed scanner in a single machine, a sensible solution when you have limited space. These can be economical choices as well, most selling for less than $200 in 2011 dollars—and some for less than $100. Keep in mind, however, that if the printer breaks down, you lose the use of your copier and scanner at the same time. If your business will be dependent on the consistent functionality of any one of these items, buy that as a stand-alone peripheral.

Scanners

A flatbed scanner—one in which you place a flat document on a horizontal glass, close the lid and press the scan button—seems like the best choice for most businesses, particularly if you find yourself scanning client materials from books or brochures on a regular basis. These can be useful for scanning photo prints as well, and some come with film scanner attachments that allow you to scan negatives or slides to your hard drive. You may need this if you're cleaning up a client's photo archives, writing a corporate history with a lot of photos and old documents to scan, or working with a lot of maps or other large, flat items.

In this age of electronic storage, I encourage you to think of your scanner beyond the occasional quick capture of a client's background materials. A good sheet-fed scanner can be your best friend in helping you reduce the amount of paper in your office on a regular basis. Using a sheet-fed scanner, you can create digital files of all of your receipts, bills, bank statements, and any other financial information that jams the drawers in your filing cabinets. Set aside an hour once a month and scan the whole kit and kaboodle into a digital folder named for that month and year, making everything accessible in a couple of mouse-clicks. Your accountant will thank you, as you can hand your entire year's records over to her on a DVD. The Internal Revenue Service accepts scanned receipts and statements as actual documents, so you'll never have to shuffle through boxes of old files again to find a misplaced receipt. (Just be sure to keep a copy of these files off-site on a CD or a flash drive, so you'll always know you have all of your necessary records in a safe place. A bank safe deposit box is a great place for this.)

Your Backup System

When do you need to think about backing up your data? Now, now, now! If you haven't had the experience of watching your life flash before your eyes as your laptop goes dark and then exhibits the Blue Screen of Death, count yourself among the world's most fortunate businesspeople. Don't get too comfortable with your luck, though, because it will run out one day, and you will face two possible outcomes: One, you will breathe a sigh of relief that you've got a reliable backup system for all of your critically important files. Or two, you will have to make the worst phone calls of your career, as you explain to your clients that you have lost all of their work in progress, and all of their projects that preceded them.

A backup system can take many forms today, none of which need to be expensive. Both Macintosh and Windows operating systems come with built-in backup applications that automate the process, taking digital snapshots of your entire hard drive as frequently as every hour. These systems work in the background, so you should experience minimal disruption, if any, to your natural workflow.

Backup systems need to copy your files onto an external hard drive that exceeds the size of your computer's hard drive. You can purchase such a hard drive from your favorite consumer electronics store (such as Best Buy), online from many manufacturers and discount computer peripheral sites, or from office supply stores like Staples or Office Max. Your computer's manufacturer may have recommendations for the most compatible equipment to match your desktop or laptop model.

Alternately, you can subscribe to an online storage service and back up your hard drive to the cloud, the ethereal name given to the nebulous online world in which your data becomes accessible to you any time, from anywhere, as long as you have an Internet connection. The cloud is not as new an idea as the recent emergence of the term might suggest. Many companies have stored data remotely using dial-up modems, T1 lines, and other now-antiquated technologies for decades; the difference is that it became easy for every household or home-based business to do this as the first decade of the twenty-first century drew to a close.

The process is simple: Subscribe to an online data storage service, purchasing enough data storage space to accommodate all of the files on your hard drive. Costs will vary based on the amount of storage you need, so if you'd like to back up every application, photo, song, and text file on your hard drive, you may find that you need tens of gigabytes to hold it all. Once you've chosen your cloud storage service provider, you'll use that company's website to upload your hard drive's contents for the first time—a process that will take some time, depending on the speed of your Internet connection (more on this below). The system will work automatically after that, replacing only the files that have been changed since the last backup—so the second backup may take just a few minutes, while the first one may take all night.

Like all systems, cloud storage has its pitfalls. While service providers are adamant about the cloud's vault-like security, there is always the risk of some hacker compromising the vault. The system can only back up while you are connected to the Internet, so if your computer is offline, no backup will take place. Finally, it's a good idea to check periodically to be sure that the backup is actually happening, and that all of your files are included; this spot-checking will save you a world of grief if you have somehow been bounced off the service provider's system because of a digital hiccup.

Your Internet Connection

Your Internet connection is the most important link in your business process supply chain, so its speed and reliability are worth a greater investment than they were when your house was just a home.

Your assignments, interviews, and media connections will come to you through e-mail, LinkedIn, Facebook, and even Twitter. Website discussion boards can be important tools for communicating with your clients' customers, building relationships with columnists, and keeping tabs on what's happening in your clients' vertical markets. This all gives us the opportunity to gather information and gauge the market's reaction to a news story more quickly and easily than ever before . . . but your clients will not want to pay for the extra time it takes you to use the web because your data connection is slow.

The Internet also provides some of the greatest opportunities for business growth the public relations profession has seen since the expansion of cable television. A speedier connection will be a direct business builder for your new firm, allowing you to respond to discussion comments faster, post news to a client's Facebook page seconds after it happens, or derail a discussion thread that's gone negative by providing the facts. The more you can capitalize on the worldwide social network, the more valuable you will be to your clients. Don't skimp on the conduit that helps you pump up your income.

Landline or Mobile?

Do you still need a dedicated, hard-wired phone line for your business?

When I let my landline go in 2010 and switched my business telephone number to my mobile phone, I sent out an e-mail to all of my clients to let them know I'd done so. The most common response I received was, "You mean you still had a regular phone line?"

The old-fashioned among us remember when a business run strictly from a mobile line was a liability—it made the enterprise look like a fly-by-night team of shady characters. Today, a mobile line is accepted for what it is: the easiest way for your clients and the media to reach you at any time, no matter where you work or travel.

With today's smartphones, it's more important than ever to have a mobile connection as your primary communications source. Your clients will expect to be able to reach you by text or e-mail if they can't get through by voice. Making yourself as accessible as possible will boost your business and prove your dependability to your clients, especially as you get your new PR firm off the ground.

Priority One: Must-Have PR Tools

Once you have your office set up with all of the basics, it's time to think seriously about which tools of the trade you need to acquire now, and which can wait until your cash begins to flow in as well as out. Here's a reality check on what you've got to have from Day One.

Contact Management Software

Whether you have to juggle a dozen editors' names and e-mail addresses or hundreds, you will need a system that helps you keep track of your last correspondence with each one, what was promised, and when you need to be in contact with him next.

Many PR professionals track this information in spreadsheet programs like Excel or Numbers, a perfectly acceptable way to manage names, addresses, phone numbers, and e-mail addresses if you have nothing else available. Others use an address book app like Apple's Address Book or Microsoft Outlook to keep notes on each conversation with an editor or producer. These are all workable, but they may not go far enough if you're managing a large database of media, or if you're tracking prospects for potential new business.

If you'd prefer to have a system that links with your calendar and sends you tickler messages to contact an editor on a specific date, it's time to move from the spreadsheet to a contact management application.

A good application will provide many functions that streamline your data entry as you create or update your media list. For example, many contact management apps come with a complete zip code library, so when you enter the contact's zip, the program immediately fills in the city, state, and even the area code. Spaces for notes allow you to record things like birthdays, personal information you've gleaned from conversations with editors, and their interest in specific kinds of stories. The best systems allow you to flag a contact as "warm" or "hot," highlighting these in color so they come to your attention in an instant when you launch the database. Functions like Skype dialing, reminders to make phone calls at specific times, and e-mailing within the app are all time savers that will speed your response time and increase your media hit rate.

As an added benefit, look for a contact management app that will synchronize with your smartphone contacts, so you have your media database with you wherever you travel.

You'll find many contact management apps available for either Windows or Mac, so shop online and watch all the overview videos you can find to determine which is the most effective for your purposes. Read plenty of customer reviews before you buy.

Client-Compatible Document and Photo Software

Microsoft Office is the accepted norm for documents, spreadsheets, and presentations in the working world, so you need to own it even if it's not your preferred package. If your clients are not working in the same version of Word as you, you need to save any documents you send them in the version they use, so they open with a click on your client's desktop. Ditto for photos, PDFs, and other files you send: Your clients must be able to open your files easily, and you must own whatever programs they use so that their files open with equal ease on your desktop.

This may mean that you will need to invest in software that your client uses, even if you have no other use for it yourself. If your client sends you Computer-Assisted Drafting (CAD) files that you need to insert into presentations or send out as attachments with news releases, then you need to own a CAD application that will open these files. (You may not need the royally expensive, full-service CAD program your client uses to draft product designs or architectural elevations, however. Look for a smaller app that will open these files for viewing.)

This may mean that you will make a significant investment in software at a time when you hope to function on a bootstrap budget. If you demonstrate your commitment to your clients by purchasing these programs up front, it's likely to pay off in continued business down the road.

Hands-Free Headset

We all have hands-free devices for talking on our mobile phones in the car, but you will find a headset equally convenient when you're sitting at your desk. Making dozens of media calls in succession really requires that you have both hands free as you do so, to take notes quickly and keep up with the conversation. Client meetings and long interviews by phone are far more comfortable as well if you don't have to hold the phone to your ear. When you shop, look for headsets with noise-cancelling capability and a clear microphone, to be sure your clients and media contacts can hear you as well as you can hear them.

Digital Camera

With tight communications budgets, especially for our nonprofit clients, it pays to have a high-resolution (8 megapixels or higher) digital camera available for taking photos of client events, new products, visits to the client site by government officials and other luminaries, work-in-progress projects, volunteer recognition events, or whatever other opportunities may arise. It's better to take photos of your own—even if they are not the perfectly posed shots a highly skilled (and expensive) professional might take—than to have an event end with no shots of grinning volunteers or grateful grant recipients. A high-end point-and-shoot camera will take photos that are more than acceptable for posting on websites and sending to online media; set the camera to shoot at its highest resolution (300 dpi is required for print) to give yourself the most flexibility when you crop and adjust the photos.

Photo editing software for your computer will allow you to do all the things the professional photo labs used to do: red-eye removal, color correction, white balancing, brightness and contrast, vignette removal, spot and patch, and a great deal more. Apple's Aperture, Corel PaintShop Pro, Adobe Photoshop, and several free programs including Google's Picasa, GIMP, Paint.NET, Photoscape, and Ultimate Paint all provide the tools you need to edit your photos.

Voicemail

Toss that answering machine you bought in 1985 and sign up for your landline phone company's voicemail service, even if it costs you a few extra dollars a month. Voicemail provides the crucial benefit of universal accessibility, allowing you to pick up your messages anywhere at any time by calling a central phone number. This service comes with your mobile service, with the added benefit of an alert signal that flashes when you have a message. No matter what kind of business you run, there's nothing more important than responding as quickly as possible when a client calls.

Priority Two: Tools for Growth

As you begin to grow your business and you take on a range of clients, new needs will reveal themselves over time. Here are some tools that can have significant value.

Media Directory, Tracking, and Distribution Service

One of the most expensive tools of the PR trade is the massive media directory, the big book of cross-referenced names, addresses, phone numbers, e-mail addresses, personal preferences, and other relevant details from which we build media lists for our clients.

In the old days, we purchased a set of these hefty, hard copy volumes on an annual basis, and received printed updates from the publishers every month or quarter. Enter the information age when we said goodbye to the fat, heavy books of contacts and began to access the directories online. Today we can not only access copious details about every editor, writer, producer, director, or media personality we want to reach, but we can also gather information on social media contacts, pull up editorial calendars for any trade magazine we wish, and track all of that activity online. We can even generate lists to which we can send news releases and other announcements by e-mail in a couple of clicks, with the certainty that these releases will make it through media spam filters to reach the targeted writers, editors, and producers.

That's the good news. The bad news is that all of this proprietary information is frustratingly expensive for home-based public relations professionals. Cision, one of the most comprehensive of these services, can run well over $2,500 annually for a subscription. Vocus, arguably the market leader in the media database game, offers a very limited membership for small businesses for which access to the media database is an add-on. Its next level, the Professional Edition—with a comprehensive list of services including contact management, media tracking, and automated reporting as well as the media database—can run up to $6,000 per year as of this writing. You may find this reasonable if you are creating new media lists on a regular basis and charging clients for the value of the information (see "What to Charge" in chapter 6), but it may be over the top as your business gets off the ground.

Here's some more good news: There are lots of sources online that can provide at least the basic information you need for free, if you're willing to invest the extra time it will take to use them. Newspapers.com, for example, provides a searchable database with a link to every major newspaper and many smaller papers throughout the United States and around the world.

If you're working in the trades or in one specialized field, professional association websites often provide links to magazines, discussion boards, websites, and other online sources that accept editorial content. If a subscription to a major media directory service is cost-prohibitive for you (as it is for most of us), you can assemble a comprehensive media list in the space of a few hours of diligent online research—and the time you spend to do this is legitimately billable to your client.

Video Calling Capability

Do you Skype (or do you use FaceTime, iChat, or Windows Live Messenger)? If not, it's time to start, especially if you have clients in distant cities or if inclement weather could keep you from attending a meeting across town.

Getting started with video chat is easy: You need a webcam—a tiny camera that sits on top of your computer monitor. Choose one with a microphone, unless your computer already has one installed. Many perfectly functional models run less than $50. (Some laptops and tablets come with a built-in video camera, so check to see if yours has this before you buy more gear.) It makes sense to buy forward and pick up a high-definition (HD) webcam, as the industry is moving quickly in this direction. HD costs a little more, but it will lengthen the usable life of your camera.

With the webcam in place, choose the video calling software that is compatible with your system, and that will work with your clients' software. Just as Microsoft Word won't open documents made in Apple Pages, Skype doesn't make calls to Windows Live Messenger or iChat; all users have to have the same program. Check with your clients to see which they use before you wed yourself to one application or another. If each of your clients uses a different video-calling app, you may need to own and become comfortable with several apps to accommodate all of them.

Happily, your investment can be rather small. Skype (www.skype.com) and Windows Live Messenger (http://explore.live.com/home) are free downloads. iChat comes with your Apple computer's operating system, and Apple's FaceTime is just 99 cents at the iTunes App Store.

Digital Voice Recorder

Some of us can do an interview and capture it word-for-word by typing it as our interviewee talks, eliminating the transcription step. For mere mortals, however, a digital voice recorder does what our tape recorders did for decades, with a twenty-first century benefit: It produces a downloadable audio file that's ready for transcription and electronic storage.

You'll find many options in digital voice recorders, so check system requirements and online reviews before you buy. Your choices may be narrowed by compatibility with Mac or PC—there are only a couple of Mac-compatible digital recorders available, and they tend to be a little more expensive than their PC counterparts.

If you do most of your interviews over the phone, SpyVille.com has a remarkable selection of digital recorders that will record your conversation right to your PC. Many of these are in the same price range as any other digital recorder.

FTP Site

If you and your clients transfer a lot of large files between you or to the media—like photos and design files—you will improve your efficiency and save yourself and your recipients a great deal of aggravation if you create a File Transfer Protocol (FTP) site, or if you choose a file transfer service.

An FTP site allows you to upload a folder or photos, design files, CAD drawings, renderings, or any other large file without compressing it, and leave the files up on the site for clients and media to access. At their convenience, clients and media can download the files they need, using an FTP client program like SimpleFTP, Fetch, FileZilla, SmartFTP, Interarchy, or a number of others. They can also upload photos and other large files to you, saving them the trouble of compressing files or mailing you DVDs filled with photos.

If the process of setting up an FTP site taxes your limited technical savvy, try a service that takes care of all the hard stuff for you. DropBox (www.dropbox.com), for example, is a free service to which you can upload up to 2GB (you can pay a small monthly fee for additional storage space) of materials to share with others. While the service was developed as cloud backup for your entire hard drive, you can create folders that are open to those you designate as users.

Virtual Meetings

Online meeting apps like GoToMeeting, GlobalMeet, Zoho, and Fuze Meeting make it possible for you to meet with clients, share the same visuals, and exchange information virtually—so you can make presentations to clients in another city from your computer. If you specialize in a certain industry and your clients are far-flung across states or even in other countries, virtual conferencing can be an invaluable confidence-builder, showing your clients that you can communicate with them as smoothly as you could if you were in the same room.

How much money will you need to set up your home office? This worksheet will get you started with the must-haves and the might-needs on your list.

Set this up as a spreadsheet in Excel or Numbers (or whatever program you use), as illustrated below. Place the cost of each Item in the column that represents the time frame in which you plan to make the purchase: Now, 6 Months, 1 Year, 18 Months, and Ongoing. Create a formula to total each of these columns, so you can see the size of the expenditure at each milestone.

Item	Now	6 Months	1 Year	18 Months & Ongoing
Room conversion				
Desk				
Chair				
Office supplies				
Computer				
Printer				
Scanner, flatbed				
Scanner, sheet-fed				
Backup system				
Internet service				
Landline phone				
Mobile phone				
Phone service				
Contact management software				
Document software				
Photo software				
Headset				
Digital camera				
Voicemail				
Webcam				
Media directory service				
Other reference materials				
Digital voice recorder				
FTP site				
Meeting software				
Other (tools germane to your business)				
TOTAL				

Boundaries and Other Fantasies

What do you believe that working from home will be like? I can tell you what others think when they're on the outside looking in: They think it's a flexible, stress-free existence in which you pursue the projects that interest you most, you put down your work when your children arrive home from school, and you're always able to take time out for a cup of coffee with a couple of pals when they have a day off from their traditional, show-up-somewhere-else-every-day jobs.

If you're that person on the outside looking in, longing for the freedom and flexibility of working from home . . . what I'm about to reveal may be a bit of a shock.

It's not like that.

Being your own boss does *not* mean that no one tells you what to do. In any client-centered business, the client rises to the level of royalty, and every command he or she bestows becomes the directive that you must follow. If you have a client who starts every day by arriving at his desk at 6:00 a.m., chances are good he'll be looking for you shortly thereafter. If your client doesn't really get revved up until after 8:00 p.m., and just starts looking at the work you sent that day when he's settled at his desk at 9:00 p.m., expect to get calls then. It's up to you if you take calls at these hours (that's what Caller ID is for), but the calls will come. If your client's got a rush job that he deposits on your desk on Friday at 4:00 p.m. and he needs the completed work back by Monday at 9:00 a.m., you'll be spending a long (and profitable) weekend on a rush project.

If you're on vacation in Glacier National Park, for example, and your voicemail signal goes off when you pass through the tiny zone with cellular service, you won't have the luxury of dodging that message. There's no junior account executive or support staff to whom you can hand over the problem; you're on your own, and to keep your clients, you need to respond regardless of your other plans for the day. Let's say the message reveals that your client needs you to solve a sticky problem he's created with someone in the media. Now you'll need to scramble to find Wi-Fi or 4G in the obstinately remote Columbia Mountain range, where people go to escape these modern conveniences, so you can swap written responses with your client and the reporter until the problem is solved. Your family may fume as they wait for you to finish and rejoin their fun, because they can't really comprehend the thrill you get from tackling these kinds of issues, even if it does take a few hours—billable hours, by the way—out of your vacation time.

For most PR people, scenarios like these are just part of the job—we knew when we founded our home-based businesses that these situations would emerge more frequently than not. When we worked in someone else's organization, however, our families did not see all of this intensive activity. Generally, our spouses and children really believe that our working from home will be less demanding than our traditional job, which took so much time away from family activities.

In that traditional office we left behind, we had to answer to our employer about time we needed away from work to take care of family. In your home-based office, you have the opposite problem: You may find that you need to answer to your family about the working time you need that takes you away from them.

How do you cope? Here are some solutions for establishing some basic boundaries.

Your Spouse's Support

Unless your spouse or significant other (I'll use "spouse" alone for the sake of brevity) also works from home, chances are you'll encounter expectations about what you can do during the workday, because your workplace is now in the same building as your residence.

Your spouse may arrive home from his or her job at the end of the day and react to the condition of the house. He or she may assume that because you're in the house all day, you should be able to wash the dishes, do the laundry, vacuum the living room rug, and put away the kids' toys. Instead of doing these things, you've billed ten hours to clients by writing news releases, talking to media, writing blog entries and Facebook posts, and outlining a three-year communications strategy for your biggest client. In the process, you completely lost track of time, so there's no dinner on the table either—not that you promised to start dinner.

It's not that your exasperated spouse doesn't appreciate that you're working. What you have here, to paraphrase the Captain in *Cool Hand Luke,* is a failure to set proper expectations. Working from home is just that: working. When your business gets rolling and you have plenty of client work coming in, your workday may vary little from the time you spent when you worked for someone else—especially because you don't have the support staff you may have had before.

Set this expectation well before your first day at home, when you start talking with your spouse about founding your own business. For the sake of family harmony, he or she needs to understand that you have the same professional workday as before, and while this does not preclude you throwing in a load of laundry at lunchtime, you won't be giving up billable time to keep house during the day. Whatever arrangements you had for cleaning and cooking before will need to continue, which means that your spouse probably needs to play a role in taking care of the household as well.

Equally difficult—and this goes for both men and women—you will need to resist the urge to spend your day cleaning the house, working on that project in the garage, picking up after your kids, or whatever other sirens call to you from the kitchen, living room, laundry room, bedrooms, and other areas of your house. There's a natural tendency to feel that everything in the house must be in place before we can work with a clear head. *This will never happen.* Learn to close your office door and shut out whatever chaos you feel lies beyond, or the siren's call will be your professional undoing.

Establishing Work Hours

Many years ago, when I spent a summer break from college scooping ice cream at a local eatery, my boss pointed out a similar confection parlor down the road that had just gone out of business. "You know what their problem was?" he said. "They didn't keep regular hours. I'd see it all the time—people would show up there, and it was closed. There were no hours posted on the door. Didn't make sense."

Regular hours establish a sense of trust and dependability that lets your clients know you are available to them when they need you. Whether you choose the fairly standard 8:00 a.m. to 5:00 p.m. schedule, or you choose to conduct your business with a later start or end time, your clients know exactly when they can access your services.

Your clients' work schedules will influence the hours you set for your business as well. If, for example, you serve clients in the live entertainment industry, you may need to shift your schedule to a later start and end time to more closely match their evening performance schedules and late-evening availability. If all of your clients are in municipal utilities, a very early start time might be the best fit with their daily routine. Those clients we mentioned earlier who like to start very early or who just get their motors running after dark are likely to call or e-mail you regardless of your stated hours, but most will respect your time as they would expect you to respect their own, and they will be happy to work within your allotted time frame.

Best of all, your family will know exactly when you are working, a guideline they can come to take seriously.

Setting Boundaries with Children

How do you tell a two-year-old child that Mommy or Daddy is too busy working to play right now?

When your little one crumples into tears just as you're starting a conference call with a group of clients, you may feel that you're embarrassing yourself if you excuse yourself from the call to remove your sobbing toddler.

While you may inconvenience your clients for a couple of minutes, the fact is that they know you're working from home—and as we discussed in chapter 1, what was once an anomaly has now become an accepted norm. Clients are much less likely to be offended by the occasional interruption from your kids.

That's all fine from the professional side, but how do you set that boundary with your children—especially those who are too young to understand?

Any parent will tell you that toddlers and business don't mix. If you're working from home and your children are home with you all day, parenting must be your top priority. This may mean that you delay your growth plans for your business until your children are in school and you have several hours at a stretch to perform client work.

Alternately, if you can afford to do so, look at daylong child care options that will keep your young children safe in a happy, comfortable environment during the day.

When your children reach school age, they are likely to demand your attention when they arrive home at the end of the day. The time from the arrival of the school bus until after dinner may turn out to be your prime time with them, especially if they have many after-school activities that require them to have transportation, or if you want to attend their events.

You can set these timing guidelines with clients if you choose—and you can choose clients who are willing to work within your limited daily schedule (especially those who are also involved parents). Not every client will take kindly to the idea that you will not be at your desk from 3:00 to 6:00 p.m. every day, but if this kind of flexibility is critical to your happiness, keep looking for the clients who will work with you on this.

As your children become old enough to understand the difference between work time and play time, it will be easier to extend your work hours and set boundaries at home. Closing your office door, placing a sign on the door that says "Busy until 4:30," and setting children's expectation that you will not be available when they get home are all viable strategies with older children.

From the Field

Barbara Haig, President, Haig/Jackson Communications

HANGING UP ON THE WHITE HOUSE

Barbara Haig knew she'd turned a corner as a home office professional when her infant son interrupted her phone call with the White House Press Office.

"I was applying for press credentials to shoot some video in the White House," she said, "when my younger son woke up and was crying. It was 18 years ago, and no one worked from home at that time. And it was the White House—I couldn't say, 'My son is crying and I have to get off the phone!'"

Instead, she made a risky move: Without a word, she simply hung up. "I ran downstairs, took care of my son, and then I called them back," she said, laughing. "I said, 'Gee, we must have been disconnected.'"

The quick bit of improvisation worked—and it became just one more tale of Haig's ability to juggle a successful communications consulting business in a home office in Milwaukee, Wisconsin, while raising two sons.

Haig came to PR through her work as a television news producer, reporter, and occasional anchor on WTMJ in Milwaukee, a career she followed with three years at a public relations firm. "When my first son was born, I couldn't work the twelve-hour days at the TV station anymore," she said. "I joined a PR firm, and after the second son was born, the PR firm gave me the best maternity leave they could, but they couldn't let me work part-time."

To help her make the leap, Haig sought career counseling. "They had me describe what I was doing then, without using the words 'television' or 'news.' I told them that I wrote, I produced, I was a project manager, I liked issues. Then they had me talk about things I liked to do—what would I do all day if time and money were no object? And what did I never want to do again? Well, I didn't like the physical process of editing videotape. And I wanted the option of choosing my own projects. At the PR firm, I had to work for companies I really did not believe in. I was against what they were doing, but it was a job and I had to do it. I never wanted to do that again."

Now on her own with an office on the second floor of her family's 1914 Arts & Crafts–style bungalow, Haig works with another home-office-based colleague, Jeff Jackson, who lives twenty miles away. Haig/Jackson Communications serves clients in the fields of energy and sustainability, as well as businesses that require outsourced corporate communications and spokesperson training. "We work with highly intelligent people, physicians and engineers who have a lot going on in their minds but they can't get it out of their mouths," she said. "Once people understand that we really are good at understanding complex concepts and boiling them down to a simple level, the work is always there."

Haig's experience extends to media relations for orchestral musicians' unions across the country, as well as PR for major corporations including Milwaukee-based Johnson Controls.

Even with such a blue-ribbon clientele, Haig made the commitment to work vs. family boundaries early, establishing personal ground rules that she and her husband (who is also self-employed, though he maintains office space elsewhere) stuck to from the beginning.

"The boys were in day care when they were little," she said. "But when they were at home, I really tried to be home with them. Voicemail was my best friend. Caller ID is great—I can look at it and see if I need to take that call now, or if it can wait. When they were in school, I always tried to be home when they got home."

With one son in college and the other already graduated and working, Haig has fond memories of being an at-home working mother and the unusual experiences she could enjoy, like the Halloween party she attended with her sons at their day care center at the Milwaukee County Courthouse. "We went trick-or-treating through the offices of the courthouse, so I visited the county executive with my kids," she said. "After that, I went home, changed my clothes, and went back to the courthouse to meet with the county executive about a musicians' union issue. I just smiled all day."

04

Writing a Business Plan

So you've just been sprung from the restrictive corporate straitjacket or from a blood-pressure-boosting agency machine, and you never, ever want to sit through one of those navel-gazing meetings about company mission, vision, and objectives ever again.

Why, then, am I about to tell you to start thinking about your mission, vision, and objectives?

It may be hard to fathom as you stand looking at the vast, inviting expanse of your career from this day forward, but you'll have a far better chance of getting where you want to be if you know where you're going. Take the time now, before you start approaching clients, to determine what your company is about, what kinds of work you want to do, and what rewards you want—beyond the money, which is a given—from being a business owner.

Even if you're picking up this book after being in business and building a solid client base, it's still the perfect time to put together a business plan. The time you spend thinking about what your business is now, what you'd like it to be five years from now, and what it will take to get there will make a difference in your ability to actually achieve your goals.

I didn't create a business plan in my first year in business—in fact, I had entered my third year when it suddenly seemed like a good idea to step back and consider my progress to date. In my first two years, I took advantage of the dot-com boom and rode the technology wave, tripling my income over my agency days with web-based clients with nebulous descriptors like "application service provider," "strategic web developer," and "certified solutions consultant." When the bottom dropped out of this market in early 2001, these clients crashed into non-existence—and I suddenly had plenty of time to consider the long-term viability of my business objectives.

I spent two weeks analyzing my target markets and writing my business plan, and I've stuck to that document ever since. Had I done this analysis at the outset, I still may have ridden the dot-com wave until it crashed on the shore, but I would have had the advantage of the multiple streams of income I outlined in my business plan.

Your business plan can be as valuable to you as the GPS device on the dashboard in your car. You decide the final destination and the vehicle in which you will travel, and the business plan does the rest, helping you determine which route will be the fastest, the shortest distance, or the most scenic. Should you decide to change destinations or add more stops along the route, plug these into the business plan as well, and adapt your route accordingly. When roadblocks require significant detours, you can change direction quickly, because you know where you want to be in the end and when you plan to get there.

Beyond the conceptual advantages, a business plan serves an important practical purpose. Should you decide to expand beyond your home office, you may need to approach a financial institution or investors for the capital you need to get going. Any bank or venture capital firm will want to see your business plan and measure your progress against it. If you do the work now, you will be ready to move as your pace accelerates.

Thinkpoint

There's no set-in-stone format for a business plan, but it's worthwhile to delve into these topics:

- Your Company: Definition, purpose, and goals
- Operating Plan
- Service/Product Plan
- Financial Plan
- Marketing Plan
- Earnings and Growth Forecast

Define Your Company

You've chosen a company name, but what do you want that name to mean to those who see it online or on your business card? This may be the toughest part of the plan to write, because you're thinking not only about what your firm is today, but what you ultimately want to become.

From the outset, try to avoid the grandiose words and lofty claims that often find their way into vision statements. Think of this process as a conversation with yourself, a realistic assessment of your strengths, the areas in which you can have the most impact, and the kind of business you want your firm to become.

Key questions:

- What kind of company do I want to run?
- Who are my clients today, and what kinds of clients do I want to target?
- What strengths do I bring to the table for my potential clients?
- If I were a client, why would I hire this company?
- Do I want to work independently for the long term, or do I want my company to grow beyond my home office and my own capabilities?
- What makes me different from other PR businesses in my area?

Know What Clients You Want

We talked in chapter 2 about being a generalist versus a specialist. Here in your business plan, you will explore these concepts to better understand your own strengths, and what your areas of expertise will offer your potential customers.

Even if you do want to leave yourself open to any kind of client that comes your way, you have areas of specialization that make you unique, and that differentiate you from your competition. It's time to add up your skills and expertise and make these qualities meaningful to the clients you plan to attract.

We're starting down the track toward discovering your *unique selling proposition*, the thing that makes you different from and better than your competition. The shorter and more concisely you can make your statement about your exemplary capabilities, the more effectively you will be able to express this to your prospects and clients.

Key questions:

- What strategic advantages do I offer my clients?
- What is my greatest area of expertise?
- What other expertise and skills make me stand out from the PR pack?
- How will my clients benefit from their relationship with my company?
- At which public relations tactics do I excel?
- What kinds of PR activities do I most enjoy doing?
- What client needs can I fulfill most effectively?
- How can I make a compelling case to potential clients that I am the right match for their needs?

Vertical Markets: A Wonderland of Opportunities

Determining what you can offer your clients will take you much closer to understanding which clients are right for you. We talked about specialization in chapter 2, and this is where it comes into play. You may have comprehensive knowledge of a vertical market—an industry category chock-full of businesses that need to talk to one another or to consumers about their products and services.

Let's take an example. Several years ago, I had a client in the theater technology industry, a very specialized vertical market. I had some professional background as a theater technician early in my career, and my husband is a lighting designer for several area theaters, so I went in with a working knowledge of this client's products.

I worked with this client for three years, during which the company introduced a revolutionary new product. At the end of the three years, this company had had so much publicity for their new product that it made the company attractive to a buyer, a much larger competitor. In that moment, it seemed that I had lost a good client, and I would need to start looking for business to replace it.

The first place I looked was in the enormous field of theater technology. Here I was with this specialized expertise in an industry-leading product. Why let that go to waste? I got in contact with my favorite editors in the technical theater trade magazines, and let them know that I was in the market for more clients in the field.

I also began to research other options in theater technology. The list was almost endless! I'd been working in rigging, but I knew all the editors who also covered lighting, sound, staging, effects, automation, audio-visual, rental companies, tour outfitters, and more. There were literally hundreds of companies I could explore and pitch for business. In just three months, I had replaced my former client with two new ones—including my original client's number one competitor. I have the pleasure of continuing to work with editors with whom I formed relationships nearly a decade ago, and I've broadened my reach within a market I enjoy.

When you understand the magic of vertical markets, you can walk through a prospect's door with a clear understanding of his or her industry and the challenges you can help this client overcome. With one or two previous clients in a vertical market, you already know more than 99 percent of the other agencies that might try to pitch your target prospect.

Which vertical markets can you begin to plumb for business? Here's a worksheet to help you figure it out.

How Big Is Your Vertical Market?

1. Create a table in your word processing program.
2. Put the title of your target vertical market at the top of the page. For example, let's say the vertical market is "Cosmetics."
3. Segment the market using the columns in the table. Make each segment a column heading. Continuing with our Cosmetics example, your column headings will say, "Skin Care," "Hair Care," "Nail Care," "Foundation Products," "Lip Care," "Eye Makeup," and so on.
4. Go to your favorite trade magazine's website in this market. Look for the list of advertisers, or the directory of services—wherever you can find a list of the companies that provide products or services to consumers or businesses in this market. If you have hard copies of the magazines, flip through them to look at the advertisements.
5. Start listing the names of these companies under the appropriate column headings in your table. It won't take long before you fill up columns and need to go to a second sheet, and even beyond that. You may need to add more columns as you discover niches in this industry that you didn't know existed.

Now you have a starting place, a long list of potential clients that you can research to find the best fit for your new business. You can narrow these down according to location, company size, the long-term viability of their products, or whatever criteria you establish as you examine the market.

The Generalist's Dilemma

In the heady early days of your business, when you're just beginning to build momentum and your friends, family members, former clients, and former coworkers are referring new clients your way, it's easy to slip into the "general PR" category and take on any kind of client, regardless of their congruity with your personal vision for your company.

There are plenty of good reasons to do this, not the least of which is your need for an income. It may seem risky to stick to your areas of expertise and specialization when you haven't made enough money to take your first paycheck out of the business yet. I started out as a generalist for just that reason, and most home-based PR practitioners do the same.

Now, with 20/20 hindsight on my side, here's why generalization is not a stepping-stone to the specialization that will truly grow your business.

First, you're always dealing with bandwidth issues. Having many different kinds of clients can keep every day fresh and unpredictable, but when you're bouncing between the fast-paced retail event world and the more structured regularity of corporate clients, things begin to fall through the cracks.

Second, you have no cogent reason to turn down accounts you know you don't want. Specialization allows you to tell Uncle Jake that you really wouldn't be the right person to do publicity for his brother-in-law's dog grooming business (unless you do specialize in pet care services), or that you don't want to write flyers for your sister's taekwondo instructor, and certainly not in exchange for free classes. If you can say, "Thank you for thinking of me, but my expertise is in the high-end fashion industry, so it's not a good fit," then you're off the hook, simply and cleanly.

If you do plan to offer general PR services to any client you can find, consider specializing in a geographic market. Your knowledge of one specific area—your home town, city, or state, for example—will make you very effective in generating media impressions and grassroots publicity for clients in that market. You will know all the media outlets and you may already have relationships with many of them, and you'll know what tactics work for your area's audience, and which have fallen flat for the clients of other firms. Whether you're working for a high-end homebuilder or a travel agent, both are looking to reach the same kind of audience in the same geographic area. This may make generalization both worthwhile and effective as a revenue stream for your new business.

How You'll Make Money: Your Services

Now that you have an idea of which markets you plan to target, it's time to determine the services you can offer your new clients.

Public relations services, by definition, include anything and everything that relates to a client's image—from brand identity to the way the client comports himself/herself in public. You have the opportunity to put every bit of your expertise to work to help your clients present themselves and their companies to the world in the most positive and professional manner, even under the most extreme duress.

Here are some of the activities you may choose to offer:

- **Media relations.** The bread and butter of the PR business, media relations are what most of us do best: We are the keepers of the golden key to the publicity door. The ability to compile a list of media relevant to the client's needs and craft the winning pitch separates good PR people from pretenders.
- **News release writing.** PR people are almost always skilled writers, so this may be a standard arrow in your company's quiver.
- **Ghostwriting.** Writing a news release is one thing, but taking a complex subject and boiling it down to 500–1,500 words for publication in a trade magazine or on a top website is quite another. If you have this skill, either because of your journalism background or from other previous experience, you will have more work than you can handle a great deal of the time. Many clients have brilliant points of view to share with their industry, but they don't possess the skill to verbalize these ideas coherently in writing. You may find yourself writing for CEOs of major corporations, university presidents, captains of manufacturing, financial gurus, and a wide range of others. My own ghostwriting credits include articles in everything from *Locksmith Ledger* to *Lighting & Sound America,* most of these bylined in print by clients. If you can check your ego at the door and enjoy the clip even without your name on it, you will make money with this skill.
- **Speechwriting.** Crafting the message for clients often means putting actual words in their mouths. Good speechwriters can charge top dollar for their services, and if the client maintains a high profile and speaks regularly on a wide range of topics, you can form a symbiotic relationship that will last throughout the client's career. Get comfortable with Microsoft PowerPoint or another presentation application, and create the appropriate visuals when the speech warrants this support.

- **Newsletter writing.** While few clients still produce a paper newsletter, many send these communications online—and they still need as much intelligently written, lively content as they ever did. Nothing aggravates an in-house communications department like the grind of having to produce a four- to eight-page newsletter every quarter, so freelance PR people become important outsourced partners in the process. Your ability to interview article sources, gather information, and speak the client's industry-specific language will make you invaluable, all while generating predictable work on a set annual schedule.

- **General communications writing.** Fundraising letters and brochures, informational websites, marketing collateral, employee communications, letters for corporate executives, workbooks, training manuals, and a host of other projects all require professional, persuasive writing skills. There is no end to the possible assignments that you can pursue.

- **Strategic communications planning.** It's one thing to execute a lot of tactics, but it's quite another to bring all of these activities together in a cohesive, carefully choreographed public relations plan. If you have a head for strategy and you can see the larger picture beyond today's emergency or next month's announcement, you can work with your clients to create a plan with projected outcomes and measurable goals.

- **Social networking.** So many clients mount a Facebook page or open a Twitter account and expect the heavens to open up and rain down loyal fans and followers, regardless of whether they ever look at the pages again or post a status update or tweet. You can help them be part of the online conversation by taking over these pages for them, working with your clients to come up with relevant content, and posting it to their Facebook page or tweeting regularly.

- **Blogs.** Plenty of clients start blogs with the intention of posting new entries regularly, but all too many blogs languish after the first couple of posts. You can remedy that situation for your clients by taking over this writing for them. Learn their industry so well that you can write for the blog on your own, or set up regular times to interview your clients by phone or in person, as they prefer. One interview might generate enough material for four or five blog entries—and you get to charge your hourly rate for writing each one.

- **Monitoring the online image.** Thanks to Google and other search engine tools, it's easy to find out what people are saying online about your client's products, services, talent, or reputation. Checking the online buzz can be an ongoing, evergreen job for you as you ferret out the gossip, discover thrilled or disappointed customers, and see where your client may want to clear up a misunderstanding or make good on a broken promise. Your work can also put a stop to rumors before they get out of hand, by allowing your client to respond to misinformation as it emerges.

■ **Monitor discussion boards.** Vertical markets often have online discussion boards on which members can talk about anything that comes to mind, as long as it relates to the overall topic. Participants often ask each other for advice about specific product issues, or about problems that one of your client's products may be able to solve . . . if only the client knew the question had been asked. You can help by finding and monitoring these discussions, and bringing relevant subjects to your client's attention in time for him to make a useful contribution to the conversation.

■ **Crisis communications.** If you have the expertise to handle a client's crisis and navigate the turbulent waters of high-stress, adrenaline-fueled communications, you can become a sought-after specialist with this capability. Whether your client made a terrible error or an unexpected disaster requires a measured, well-considered response, your services will be among the most valued assistance the client receives. In my career, I've handled the aftermath of a murder in an affordable apartment complex owned by my nonprofit client, a potential exposure to tuberculosis in a day care center, the cancellation of a major star's appearance at a highly publicized event, the death of a key partner in an accounting firm, and any number of industrial gaffes that required more than a quiet letter of apology. This is fertile, profitable territory for PR specialists.

■ **Media training.** If you've got a great deal of on-camera experience, you can train others to be as smooth and polished as you are when talking to the media. It only takes one silly mistake for a client to decide that he or she really needs to learn to handle an interview more intelligently. (My personal favorite: A colleague running for office jokingly told a reporter that he launched his campaign when his six-year-old daughter, for whom he'd been a stay-at-home dad since her birth, had asked him, "Daddy, when are you going to get a real job?" When that quote made him an object of ridicule, he decided to seek media relations advice. Sadly, it was too late to salvage his campaign.)

These are just a few of the services you may choose to offer your clients. List the ones most appropriate for you in your business plan.

Key questions:

- What services are most in my area of expertise?
- What kinds of services will my target clients need most?
- What kinds of activities do I most enjoy?
- What have I done in the past that I never want to do again?
- How can I capitalize on the trends in the industry that have created (or will create) new opportunities for public relations professionals?

From the Field

Christopher Budd Communications (christopherbudd.com)

"The goal was to be more sane."

"Ten years at Microsoft is a long time," said Christopher Budd from his home office outside of Seattle, Washington. "I was in one of the highest-stress areas of what is already a high-stress company."

It was Budd's job to manage worldwide internal and external communications around security and privacy incidents affecting Microsoft Corporation customers—an awesome responsibility that placed him at the epicenter of every crisis. "I have a very rare skill set— you can count on one hand the number of people who have managed online security and privacy crises," he said. "Most mainline PR people will manage one or two major crises in their lifetimes. I've managed one or two a month for years."

Early in 2011, Budd and his wife (who also works for Microsoft as a documentation manager) came to the conclusion that enough was enough: It was time for the couple to diversify their income, and for Christopher to take control of his schedule and his future. He resigned from Microsoft with the goal of becom-

---

ing a consultant, offering his specialized services to the vast field of companies facing privacy and security crises of their own.

First, however, he did little but sleep for several weeks.

"In crisis response, you're on call 24/7/365," he said. "So there was a lot of recovery time. But after sleeping, the first thing I started to do was self-promotion and marketing, building up an online presence." Budd built a website for his new company, with the provocative slogan, "Helping you make awful news just bad." His active blog provides his expert views on all manner of brand identity issues, from the Netflix/Qwikster botch-up to methods for using social media to remedy bad situations. Not surprisingly, he's got a command of online media and tools that places him among the social media elite.

Networking in person, however, took more effort than he initially realized. "Microsoft is an environment that envelops people," he said. "When I started to think about leaving, I looked at LinkedIn and I had sixty contacts—and most of them worked at Microsoft. Now I have more than five hundred. One of the first things beyond that was a Public Relations Society (PRSA) group event where three independent practitioners gave a talk on what they had done. That was valuable from a nuts and bolts point of view. Then I started engaging with the local chapter of PRSA; I got myself on the events committee. That was a good opportunity to start meeting peers outside of Microsoft."

Before long, Budd's contacts among people who had left Microsoft were the first to come through with business for him. His first client was a former colleague who had moved to another major technology company; the relationship resulted in a thirty-hour-a-week contract for a full year. The arrangement allows Budd to work from home on a company laptop, then close up the Windows-based machine and take out his personal MacBook for his business development work. "My wife got it for me as a bit of quiet rebellion," he said.

With the luxury of a three-quarter-time job already in hand, Budd can take the time to do things he and his wife had put off for a decade. "Our home is surrounded on three sides by a state park," he said. "I'm sitting on my porch right now surrounded by two-hundred-foot fir trees. In June, we started a massive home remodel inside—that's finished, but we don't have all our furniture back yet. So my office is a lap desk in the den. Definitely not advisable! We have a loft area with a large desk, and I'll set that up as my work area. But my job over the summer was getting the construction done."

The new arrangement has trade-offs, Budd said, but he can say without question that his new life is worth the change. "The goal was to be more sane," he said. "In terms of take-home pay, I'm not making as much as I used to. We made adjustments in our living style so we could live on my wife's paycheck while I started this work. And when my wife gets home, she doesn't have to worry about the dishes. Since I'm home, I do view the maintenance of the house as primarily my responsibility in terms of oversight."

To others who are considering the leap from a corporate job with high pay and benefits, Budd advises a reality check. "Really sit down and think about if you've got the right mental posture for working on your own," he said. "In a full-time environment, there's a degree to which the initiative and the self-reliance you need on your own are not only not fostered, they're squashed. Can you make that shift, so you can move from taking orders from higher-ups to doing it all on your own? Even if you work for someone else, you can foster that sense of independent work identity, and that's just critical."

Subcontractors

Much as we would like to do everything ourselves and keep all the money, clients may require services we simply can't provide on our own. It makes good business sense to find subcontractors who can supply you with services like graphic design, video production, photography, data entry, and other creative or administrative tasks for which you do not currently have the knowledge or skills. As the head of your company, you still will supervise these projects and bill the client for the cost of the subcontracted service (plus a markup; see chapter 6 for more on this).

In your business plan, list the services for which you expect to engage subcontractors, and the people or businesses you plan to engage. These relationships become "strategic business assets" in the parlance of the economic world.

Projected Expansion

Here's the big question: Do you want to remain a one-person, home-based business, or do you have your mind set on expanding your enterprise to an agency with its own address? If expansion is your plan, how big do you want to be?

It's a tough question to answer during your first week in business when you haven't even signed your first client yet, but the decision may influence the initial structure of your firm, and it definitely will impact the way you present yourself and your new business to the world.

If you don't have any idea what you want to be in five years, that's just fine—unless you're planning to go out to investors with your business plan. Anyone who writes you a check to help you get your business off the ground will want to know what your vision for this enterprise may be, even if your investor is your spouse or your parent.

To help you determine what may be the right level of business for you, talk to others who have made this leap. Find out if those who grew their firms to large companies with many employees are happy that they did so. Chat with others who work from home, especially those who have done it for the long term, and see how they feel about their decision to stay small. Talk with boutique agency owners with five or six employees, and find out if they increased their personal profitability and satisfaction with this configuration.

You may be surprised at the responses you get, but they will help you make at least an initial decision for yourself. It's possible that even if you decide you never want the responsibility of supervising a staff, your circumstances may change as your client list grows. Keep an open mind, but choose a direction for your company at least in the short term, to help you focus on doing the right things to be successful with whatever plan you adopt.

Key questions:

- Do I want to be an employer? If so, what will that entail legally, physically, financially, and emotionally?
- What benefits will remaining an at-home business provide?
- What benefits might I enjoy if I grow the business beyond my home?
- What are the pitfalls of staying small, and of getting bigger?
- What do I miss about working for a larger company?
- What do I *not* miss?

Writing an Operating Plan

It's time to get down to the nuts and bolts of running your business.

The operating plan contains your legal structure, a list of your key advisors, your location and space requirements, your leadership, methods through which clients can pay you, and your financial picture and projected income.

You may be surprised at how refreshing it is to spell out all of these details. What feels like an exercise in minutiae actually turns into an important part of your business planning, with a focus on making sure you have the support you need to succeed.

We'll review the various legal structures available to you in chapter 5—you need to choose between becoming a sole proprietorship, a corporation, or a partnership. Each of these requires specific steps that must be taken at the outset, so you're set up properly to pay your income and corporate taxes, take in and pay state and local sales tax, and protect yourself, your family, and property should your business fall into debt or fail.

Define your leadership—that's you—and give yourself a title. If you're a sole proprietorship, "owner" may be all the title you need. Corporations require officers, so you may choose to be president, chief executive officer, or both. In partnerships, you may refer to yourself as partner or managing partner, or principal. All of these are paper titles; you can call yourself Chief Media Maven or Rockin' PR Queen on your business cards if you choose, but these titles are a little hard to explain to a bank when you're meeting with a loan officer to open a business line of credit.

List your key advisors: anyone you can call at a moment's notice to ask a question or bounce around some ideas. If you have mentors within the PR community and you have their permission to call them advisors, list them and explain the expertise they bring to your business. You may include retired PR executives from other companies, family members with useful knowledge, or friends who have been helpful to you professionally in the past. It makes sense to include a fellow at-home PR practitioner with many years' experience working at home, as he or she can really help you find your way in the early days of your business. You don't require a long list of advisors— think of these people as the friend you would phone if you needed the answer to the million-dollar question.

List your location with a brief description. It's fine to say, "Someone Public Relations will do business from my home at 123 Garden Variety Way," and leave it at that. If you have designs on an outside office a few years down the road, specify the size of the projected space and general location (i.e., "in the southeast quadrant of Rochester, New York") to give an idea of your goal.

How will your clients pay you? With the electronic options available today, you can make many choices for receiving payments beyond the traditional check or pricey credit card arrangements. We'll talk more about these in chapter 6 under the heading, "How to Get Paid."

Finally, provide a clear, numerical summary of your financial picture. How much money do you need to get started? Refer back to the worksheet on page 54 to determine the costs of setting up your home office. Now add to this the cost of marketing your new business (see chapter 10), getting your corporate identity materials in place (more on this in chapter 5), and supporting yourself until the business can provide you with a regular paycheck, and you have an idea of the money you really need today.

Compare this figure with the money you have on hand. Do you plan to finance your start-up with your personal savings? Will you borrow money from a relative, or will you approach a bank for a loan? There is nothing wrong with borrowing money to start out—in fact, this part of your business plan will present the case for a bank loan, should you choose to approach a financial institution for one. If you do not see a fairly clear path to income on your horizon, however, consider sticking with the money you have in hand to begin the prospecting process before you borrow. You will still have all of your household expenses to pay as your business moves forward, so adding a big bank loan payment to these may create a hardship situation until you land your first new accounts. (We'll talk more about this in chapter 7: "Money: How to Manage It.")

The Marketing Plan

Perhaps the most important part of your business plan, the marketing plan describes the breadth and density of your target customer base, and builds a picture of your ability to gain and keep clients. It forces you to sit down and think hard about who you want to work for, your chances of gaining access to these potential clients, and the tools you will use to get their attention, build name recognition and top-of-mind awareness, and win their business.

The good news is that you already know how to do this. Public relations and marketing often work hand in hand, and many communications professionals are proficient in both. You know which tactics are effective with audiences of many kinds, especially if you've been in an agency situation or on a corporate communications staff before your decision to form your own business. Now you can put all of that expertise to work for the most demanding and ultimately satisfying client of all: yourself.

Let's walk through the steps involved in creating your marketing plan, so you can see what familiar territory you'll cross.

Your Objectives

What kinds of clients do you want to attract? How many clients do you need to get your business to the point at which you can take a regular paycheck, pay your business expenses, and start to put money into good things like a retirement account and health insurance? Define the goals for your marketing plan based on your real-life, realistic needs. When you reach these goals, you can revise the plan for your continued growth.

Key Audiences

Who are your best possible clients, and how do you know? List the kinds of businesses, organizations, or individuals you'd like to add to your client roster. How do your skills mesh with their requirements? What makes you the best choice for their PR needs?

Key Messages to Each Audience

What do you have to say to each of these prospect categories? Here you need statements about your understanding of their challenges, based on your past experience or your general knowledge of their industry or situation. Add your passion for these markets, the strengths you personally provide (do you work very fast? are you methodical and deliberate?), and—a key differentiator—the cost of your services versus the staggering price of a larger firm. Now you have the content of your marketing messages.

Competition

Much as we would like to believe that our potential clients are standing on one foot, waiting for us to walk in their door and return them to lives of balance and harmony, we know that most of them have public relations suppliers of one kind or another who are serving their needs. They may have in-house staff members who handle their media relations and image management, or they may be using larger firms that can provide dedicated account executives who supply them with strategic PR and writing services. Or they may already be using an at-home PR provider like you.

Who are these companies? It's easy to state in your business plan that all PR firms everywhere represent your competition, but this view won't get to the heart of the competitive issue: how you will sell against them. Hill & Knowlton, Porter Novelli, Burson Marsteller, and other global PR firms may be knocking on the doors of the Fortune 500 businesses in your area, but these large corporations may not be the clients you intend to pursue.

Take a close look at the firms that serve your target markets, whether you're planning to stay local or reach out to potential clients across the country. It may be easier than you think to determine which firms are working in your niche, thanks to the power of Google and other search engines. Try searching on "PR firm for [name of client]," and see what pops up; then search on the names of other clients in the same niche. You will begin to see the same PR firm names repeatedly. These are your true competition.

Once you know your competitors by name, you can begin to build your case for your strengths compared to theirs.

Key questions:

- Do you have special expertise in this market?
- Do you have years or decades of experience in working with clients like these?
- Are you more nimble and responsive than other PR firms, because of your one-person size?
- Do you have special relationships with editors and producers in this niche?
- Are you less expensive because of your low overhead?

Strategy

The strategy is not a list of tactics; it's closer to a philosophy. It's the overarching plan that you will put into practice to achieve your objectives.

If you're not a strategy maven, think of it this way: You may already have a big list of tactics you plan to use to reach out to potential clients: online communications, direct mail, phone calls, gifts, whatever gets you through the door. But what will the theme of your messaging be, and how will you present yourself and your message to the world of potential clients? Within these elements lies your strategy.

Perhaps you plan to specialize in online communications, so you will use this technology to sell your services, restricting your communications to social networking and other electronic tools.

Or you will approach your market using a broad spectrum of vehicles to be sure to reach people in the ways in which they are most comfortable communicating: through the printed or spoken word as well as through digital means.

Key questions:

- How will you go about meeting your objectives?
- Why have you chosen the tactics you intend to use?
- How will you communicate your unique message to potential clients?
- Are you confident that your potential clients will be receptive to your approach? (If not, you need to rethink your strategy.)

Tactics

Here's the nuts-and-bolts section of your marketing plan. Create a list of all the things you plan to do to attract clients to your new business. That's the first step; now take this list and determine in what order these activities should be executed, and to which potential clients. Make each tactic part of a cohesive plan that will open doors to in-person presentations of your capabilities.

Key questions:

- How will each of these tactics carry out the strategy you detailed above?
- How do these tactics work together to bring your message to your targeted prospects?
- In what order will you do these things?
- How will you judge the success of a specific tactic?
- At what point will you know if a tactic (or series of tactics) is not working, and should be scrapped?

Earnings and Growth Forecast

To finish your business plan, set some goals that will help you benchmark your success against your real financial need for business and income. Calculate financial goals for one year from now, two years, and five years.

Key questions:

- How much money do you need to make? (We'll talk more about how to calculate this in chapter 6.)
- How many clients do you need to have to achieve this income level?
- How many clients can you serve at a time effectively?
- If you have the opportunity to serve more clients than your capacity allows, how will you maintain these clients with excellent service?
- Do you intend to become wealthy from your efforts? Or is your interest in a comfortable but different lifestyle from the one you had while working for someone else?
- Whatever your answer, how much business do you need to achieve that goal?

Now you have the rulebook, the template for the way you will go forward with your new company. Refer back to this plan as you begin to build business, to remind yourself of the ideals you put in writing at the beginning. Your goals may change over time—you may find that a specific market niche is not as viable as you hoped, or that your skills apply nicely to a market sector or kind of business you had not considered at the outset. A business plan is a living document, one you can revise as often as you like as you grow, as the market changes, or as your personal goals are altered by time and circumstance.

05

Ready, Set . . .
Start Your Business!

Setting up a small business in your home requires a certain amount of up-front legal and financial activity. You will need to file some paperwork, set up the conduit through which you pay your corporate and income taxes, and keep your home, your business, and your reputation safe should challenging times visit your firm.

Your Professional Team

Every business needs three professional service people who help you do things the right way the first time: an accountant, an attorney, and an insurance agent. In addition, you will need to form a relationship with a bank that will provide your checking account, overdraft protection, line of credit, and any other support you need.

Your Accountant

If you have the knowledge and the patience to keep your own financial records and even to file your corporate taxes, you may be able to save yourself some professional fees by doing so. Indeed, it's never been easier to track your day-to-day income and expenses, balance your checking account, and pay your bills from your desktop, thanks to user-friendly financial programs like Intuit's QuickBooks Pro and Sage's Peachtree Complete Accounting, each of which sells for under $200 (in 2012 dollars).

To set up the right financial structure for your business from the outset, however, hiring an accountant is the best route. Look for an accountant who specializes in small businesses, to keep your one-person enterprise from falling through the cracks at a large corporate tax firm.

Your accountant can help you decide what kind of entity your business should be: a sole proprietorship, corporation, limited liability corporation, or partnership. (We'll cover these in the next section below.) Most important, you will be glad for your accountant's wise counsel and skill at tax time, when you have to face the rigors of the federal and state tax code—things that are not written in language we non-financial types understand.

Your Attorney

To ensure that you create your business entity correctly and follow all of the local, state, and federal rules for doing so, your attorney becomes an important resource. He or she can help you make the most logical and advantageous choice for your business entity, and then take care of preparing and filing all of the paperwork required. Again, choose a person or firm who specializes in small businesses—your best friend may be a real estate attorney and your spouse's brother may deal in civil law, but they may not work with setting up small businesses on a regular basis. If you've never worked with an attorney before, you're well within your rights to interview several before choosing the one who will be your trusted resource. Personality can be just as important as skill in someone who will advise you on matters that affect your professional status and your personal well-being.

Your Insurance Agent

Once you establish a business in your home, your business property may no longer be covered under your homeowner's insurance policy. It's time to purchase business insurance, both to cover your computer, office furniture, and other tools against damage or theft, and to provide you with the financial cushion you would need if your office became unusable because of a natural or manmade disaster.

Business insurance offers many options, each of which addresses a certain kind of risk to your business. Deciding the level of insurance you require is best done with the combined assistance of your accountant and a qualified insurance broker. Your accountant can provide the impartial advice you need, while the broker can show you the full range of plans available to you. Keep in mind that it's your broker's job to sell you products, so it's best to come to a meeting with your broker with a well-informed, educated understanding of the insurance your business actually requires.

Here's a quick reference guide to help you become familiar with the kinds of policies you will be offered.

- **Property and liability insurance.** This covers your business property—office equipment, furniture, reference materials, and so on—in case of a fire, damage from a major storm, or any other accidental loss (if you live in a flood zone, you may need to buy additional insurance to cover losses involving flood damage). Choose a property policy that provides income during the suspension of your business while you recover from the damage. Often called "loss of use insurance," this coverage can be invaluable if it takes weeks or months to recover from a natural disaster.

    Liability insurance is critical if you will be meeting with clients in your home office. If a client slips on the ice on your front step and breaks a leg, your homeowner's insurance may choose not to cover this business visit. Your business liability insurance will pay for medical bills and any other expenses that might be involved.

- **Commercial auto insurance.** If your business owns your vehicle, you may need special insurance to cover the car for business use. Discuss this with your auto insurance provider to see if you need this additional expense.

- **Workers' compensation insurance.** This insurance protects your business if someone you employ is injured in a workplace or worksite-related accident. Your annual payroll determines the cost of the insurance, and even with you as the sole employee, the cost can be formidable. Check the laws in your state to determine if you are required to carry this insurance for your business if you are the only employee. Your health insurance will cover any injury you may sustain on the job (like carpal tunnel syndrome, for example), but only workers' comp will provide financial support if you must be out of work for some period of time because of the injury.

- **Errors and omissions (E&O) insurance.** Let's say you're representing a client as a spokesperson (in a political campaign, for example), and you make a factually incorrect statement that gets quoted in a major newspaper. As your quote gets picked up by other newspapers, websites, and the twenty-four-hour television news networks, your client not only fires you, but slaps you with a hefty lawsuit. How will you survive this trauma? If you have errors and omissions insurance, you may be able to offset the entire cost of the suit without having to dissolve your business, sell your home, or otherwise compromise your financial situation.

    Let's hope this dramatic example never happens to you; generally, home-based PR people do not find themselves in such a position. This does provide some insight, however, into why E&O insurance is often the most expensive kind of policy you can buy. When the stakes are so high that the client calls his attorney, the settlement amount and legal costs may be staggering, and your insurance company will be required to pay out hundreds of thousands or even millions of dollars. You can avoid a great deal of this risk by establishing parameters in writing with your clients at the outset, and never releasing anything to the media or the general public without approval and written sign-off (an e-mail can be considered a legal document in many cases).

That being said, if you know that you may be working in high-risk situations in which information will fly thick and fast without all the necessary approvals, E&O insurance will protect you from losing everything if you are held liable for a major error.

- **Disability insurance.** While it's not business insurance per se, disability insurance will compensate you personally if you become unable to work for an extended period because of an illness or injury. Workers' compensation will only cover you for injuries that result from a work-related accident, so if you get sick from something that has nothing to do with your hours at the computer, you could find yourself with no income until you can return to work. As valuable as it can be to you, however, personal disability insurance is extremely hard to get when you're self-employed. If you have not already done so as a matter of course, secure this insurance while you are an employee elsewhere.

- **Health insurance.** One of the largest ongoing costs of self-employment is the price of health insurance. If your spouse is employed and you can be covered under that policy, count your lucky stars and take that option. If not, brace yourself for the complex world of choosing a health insurer, understanding what will and will not be covered by the policy you can afford, and coping with the annual cost increases in even the most basic policy.

As a sole proprietor, you may find that the insurers in your area will not allow you to buy a policy directly from them. You may need to join your local chamber of commerce (for a fee) and purchase your insurance as part of their group, or find a health insurance exchange that negotiates for many small businesses as a group. As I write this, the 2010 Affordable Care Act is about to change the way small businesses buy and use health insurance, so check with your local congressperson's office or chamber of commerce to find out what is available to you.

Other Trusted Advisors

Building a team of service professionals is a necessary and vital part of establishing your business, but having people to talk with about your business strategy, your action plan for the tough times, and your ideas for growth can be every bit as valuable. Chances are good that you have mentors whose advice you respect, be they leaders in the business, other home-based PR people with many years of experience, college instructors or professors, or former clients or coworkers. Who can you call for a cup of coffee and a good talk when you're struggling with a decision? Build on the relationships you have, join a professional association, or get out there and network (see chapter 10) to meet others in your industry for a mutually beneficial mentoring relationship.

Debug: Don't Take Advantage of Your Mentors

Businesspeople love to talk about what works and what doesn't work in the changing marketplace, so it's easy to think that the sky's the limit in discussing strategies and tactics for growing a business. Expecting help with solving a client's communications challenges, however, goes beyond the boundaries of the mentoring relationship. Don't expect your advisors or colleagues to do the work for which your clients pay you. Nothing ends a good mentoring relationship faster than asking for free advice, the use of which will lead you to a fat check from your clients. If you need that kind of advice, offer to pay for an hour of your mentor's time. You may still get the consultation for free, but he or she will know that you respect and value the expertise.

Business Structure Basics

Your business must exist as an entity of its own, so you can invoice your clients, claim their payments as income, pay your taxes correctly, and otherwise operate in a legal and above-board manner. From simple to more complex, businesses can take many forms.

DBA

An abbreviation for "doing business as," the DBA is required from your first day in business. It establishes the name you will use for your company, and puts you on the local and state books, so to speak, as a business that can now charge fees for its work. With your DBA in place, you can open a business bank account (you will need to bring proof of your DBA to the bank to do this). You can file for your DBA locally in the city or county in which you live. Check online or give your county clerk's office a call to find out the procedure for filing your DBA.

Before you file your business name, do a search to be sure that no other business in your area or market already does business under this name. In most areas, you can access your county's list of DBAs online, but this may not reveal companies on a wider scale that may already have legal rights to the name you've chosen. It's easy to solve this, however: A Google search will reveal other businesses with the same or similar names. If you're not certain if a business with a similar name will be in conflict with your own, ask your attorney.

Sole Proprietorship

Many home-based businesses are automatically considered sole proprietorships, because they have only one person managing the business (you). You can hire employees and still remain a sole proprietorship, so this may be a comfortable classification for you for the long term. You make the decisions, you pay the bills, and you are responsible for the success of your enterprise. You don't need to file a separate tax return for your business, but you will need to file a Schedule C with your 1040 personal tax return to detail your business income and expenses. The total of your income minus your expenses is the personal, taxable income you record on the first page of your 1040. You will pay income taxes only on the difference between your income and your expenses.

Like all forms of business, a sole proprietorship has advantages and disadvantages. There are few papers to file, so you don't need to involve an attorney at the outset to set up your business. You can begin and end the business whenever the time is right, without going through a dissolution process, and the business has fewer government restrictions and requirements than a corporation.

On the downside, a sole proprietorship does not protect you should you find yourself the subject of a lawsuit that requires you to liquidate all of your assets, or if you default on a business loan. In such a case, a court could seize your home, car, and

> ### Debug: Income Reporting Watch-Out
>
> It may seem terrific at first to see the small amount of taxable income that remains after you've subtracted your Schedule C expenses on your tax return, because your tax liability may be quite low. Your annual income, however, determines the amount of Social Security you get when you retire—so a lower income figure each year means that you will get a smaller Social Security check after you turn 65 or 70. When you get that big income tax refund every year, you may want to invest it to make up the difference later in life.

other personal belongings. In addition, while you could leave your business assets to your heirs when you die, the business itself dies with you.

Limited Liability Company

A limited liability company (LLC) combines elements of a corporation and a sole proprietorship. As an owner, you can enjoy the liability protection a corporation offers, in that you will not be held liable for debts unless you have signed a personal guarantee that you will pay them. You don't need to file annual corporate minutes, and—most important—all of your business profits, losses, and expenses pass through the company to the individual members. This allows you to avoid the double taxation of paying corporate tax on your profits, and income tax when you distribute these profits to yourself and any partners you may have.

To form an LLC, you need to file Articles of Organization, which are much like the Articles of Incorporation you would file as an S Corp or a C Corp. There are fees associated with the filing, of course, and your attorney will charge you for the filing as well. Once you've formed your LLC, you need to elect to be federally classified as a sole proprietorship, partnership, or corporation when you file your taxes. Which one you choose will determine which federal forms you use when you file.

Partnerships

You may decide to go into business with another PR practitioner, or with someone who offers services that your clients need that you cannot provide on your own. To do this, you and your coworker can form a partnership. There's little difference between a sole proprietorship and a partnership as far as the tax code goes: You will need an employer identification number (EIN)—apply for one at the Internal Revenue Service website, www.irs.gov. You will be required to file an annual notice of revenue distribution with the IRS, noting what money was paid to each of you. As partners, you and your coworker will share the responsibility for business expenses, debts, and any judgments against you. You are both owners, so neither of you are employees of the business, and you can determine your pay structure based on whatever arrangement is best for you: a regular weekly or biweekly payment from the business, a profit sharing agreement, or another idea you may have for paying yourselves.

Like any professional situation, partnerships offer benefits and potential disadvantages. It's great to have someone who can fill in the gaps, cover for you when you need to travel for business, and become part of your team for larger jobs that require additional manpower. At the same time, you may discover that you and your partner face the same kinds of compatibility issues that break up so many marriages: differences in temperament, work habits, attitudes about money, lines of authority, and a lack of commitment to the partnership's goals.

If you plan to proceed with a partnership, you and your partner should draw up a formal partnership agreement from the outset. A thorough agreement will cover the following points:

- Your business goals and the kinds of clients you intend to pursue
- The investment in time, labor, and cash or other resources each partner will contribute to establish the business
- The salary or earnings distribution plan, including profit sharing
- Each partner's legal and financial powers with regard to withdrawing or transferring money, making spending decisions, and so on
- A clause that details the procedure should one partner exit the business or die
- How conflicts between the partners will be resolved, i.e., through outside mediation or another means
- The steps required to dissolve, update, or revise the agreement

If your new partner resists the idea of putting a written agreement in place, it's a sure warning sign that your partnership will run into problems in the future. Take this to heart: James H. Krefft of the Partnership Continuum states that almost 80 percent of all business partnerships fail, mostly because leaders overlook—accidentally or intentionally—the risks involved in forming these relationships.

From the Field

Micah Warren and Lindsey Gardner, Large Media, Inc.

COULD YOU WORK WITH YOUR SPOUSE?

Shortly after they got married in 2010, Micah Warren and Lindsey Gardner both found themselves at crossroads in their careers.

Warren had just dissolved a business partnership, and Gardner had begun freelancing when the 2008 financial crisis brought an end to her position at a Manhattan communications agency. Ready to give up the drudgery of their daily commute into New York City, they made a leap that would make many married couples recoil in terror: They went into business together.

From a one-bedroom apartment in Philadelphia, they became Large Media, Inc., a full-service public relations and marketing communications firm of two. Today, these two self-proclaimed alpha personalities work from the Doylestown, Pennsylvania, house their business success made possible. They serve an eclectic client list including top-of-the-line audio speaker and turntable manufacturers, a company that organizes fresh fruit fundraisers, and the manufacturers of Incrediwear, circulation-stimulating socks and braces.

"When we first started out, we had a desk and a phone and that was it," said Gardner. "Now we are so fortunate with a loft, a nice area with filing cabinets and storage space."

Not every husband and wife team can work together comfortably, but Warren and Gardner found equanimity in the diversity of their skill sets. Dividing up job responsibilities came naturally, said Warren. "Lindsey does bigger picture stuff—branding, social media work, and overall marketing concepts," he explained.

"Micah does the PR," said Gardner. "When we get new clients, we just feel it out. If one of us has more interest in a topic and more time to do it, that's who takes it over to start. One of us is the main contact, and the other is there for backup support and checking ideas."

While Warren usually works in the loft space, Gardner takes her laptop into the guest bedroom, living room, or the house's finished basement, giving the two agency principals the space to have their own work styles. "We've rediscovered IM [instant messaging]," said Warren. "Even with Facebook and Twitter and everything, IM has been the best for us. This is the perfect application for it."

Respecting one another's professional space extends to client business, Warren added. "If Lindsey is in charge of an account and she needs something, I have to give it to her," he said. "And the same goes for the other way around. That's what we've learned about working together."

"And if Micah needs me to do something, I do it," said Gardner. "Our system has worked out well. We don't have employees now, but if we ever need some, I don't want to get into the situation where we would have a big blowout over work. You can't do that and sit down to dinner and have everything be fine."

So far, the advantages of their combined working and domestic relationship have far outweighed any drawbacks. "The flexibility of schedule is absolutely number one," said Warren. "I can work any time of the day I want, and I can be available to my client any time of day. I've been out at midnight working with a client."

"A lot of our clients are on the West Coast, so we never see them face to face," said Gardner. "We can offer them a lower retainer every month, because we're not paying for office space."

Can it really be this idyllic? "On the negative side, every day is not great," said Gardner. "There are days that can be stressful. Sometimes I do miss communication with the outside world—sometimes we realize we haven't left the house in two days. When that happens, we'll run an errand in the middle of the day, or we'll knock off a little early and run out to a happy hour, just to see other people."

The big triumphs, however, easily outweigh the rougher days, Warren said. Like the weekend the high-end audio speaker client called in a panic from a trade show: "He'd just got to Vegas, and he said, 'I screwed up.'" Warren recounts. "They're very particular about what they play through their speakers, and his source material got left behind. So I drove up to his house in Nyack, New York, got his CDs, and shipped them off to him. He got them the next day. He knew he could get to me because I had a home office."

Corporations

If you want to create a legal separation between your personal assets and your business, you need to make your business a corporation. Incorporating your business is a legal process that requires the participation of an attorney, some fairly hefty up-front fees, and considerable paperwork both at the outset and throughout the life of your company.

What is a corporation? It's a business entity with shareholders (owners), a board of directors who are ostensibly elected by the shareholders, and officers who actually run the business. This may sound like a top-heavy, complex structure for your one-person business, and it is—but in most states, it's legal for you to be the sole officer, chairman of the board, and the sole shareholder.

As a corporation, you will file a Certificate of Incorporation or Articles of Incorporation with your state. You will need to adopt a set of bylaws—your attorney can provide some standard language for these—and hold an annual meeting of the directors and shareholders each year to share financial information, after which you will file the minutes of the meeting with the state. (Your attorney can do this for you each year as well, with the accompanying annual legal fee.)

Incorporating your business protects your personal assets from your business, so in the case of a lawsuit or a business bankruptcy, you would not have to relinquish your home, retirement savings, and other personal accounts. A corporation also may seem like a better risk to banks and other lenders than a sole proprietorship, so if you plan to borrow money to get your business up and rolling, you may want to incorporate as an early step. Even better, you can sell corporate stock to raise money if you're willing to deal with the realities of shareholders, who will expect to share your profits.

If you're hoping to sell your business when you retire, becoming a corporation will make this possible—you can sell your shares and literally cash out of the company. Finally, a corporate structure may allow you to give yourself more fringe benefits— like business ownership of your vehicle, business-paid health insurance, and retirement investment options—than are available to you as a sole proprietor.

That's the upside. Corporations also come with their share of challenges: more paperwork, higher ongoing accounting fees, the need to keep separate business accounts with significant documentation, and the need to pay taxes on your profits.

If you incorporate, you will need to choose between two basic corporate structures:

- **The C Corporation** is a separate, taxable entity that files a Form 1120 federal corporate tax return each year. Taxes are paid on the annual profits before any dividends are distributed to shareholders; if there's a profit and you distribute dividends, the shareholders are then required to pay taxes on this money again. This means that if you are the only shareholder and you distribute a dividend to yourself, you will pay taxes on the profit through the corporation first, and then again when you take it as profit from an investment. (You can take the profit as a bonus instead, but you'll pay income tax on it anyway.)
- **The S Corporation** gets its name from Subchapter S of the Internal Revenue Code, and it provides much the same benefits as a C corporation—but with some distinct differences. S corporations do not pay taxes at the corporate level. Instead, they file Form 1120S, an informational federal return, and the profits or losses from the business are reported directly on the owners' personal tax returns. This means that if the business generates a profit and taxes are due, you pay these taxes out of your own (after-tax) income.

Which form is right for you? Your accountant and attorney can help you make the decision, based on your personal circumstances, your expectation of profits, and your need to protect your own assets and distance these from your business entity.

Choosing Trusted Suppliers

With the breadth and depth of potential public relations services you can offer, you're likely to find that you can fulfill a greater range of client needs if you contract with suppliers who can perform services that dovetail with your own talents.

- A **graphic artist** can be a tremendous asset—someone who can take your expertise articles, white papers, brochure or newsletter copy, or other materials and turn them into beautiful PDFs or pieces ready for printing.
- A **website developer** can save you the trouble of learning to build websites on your own (although this process is almost as easy as word processing these days). In today's PR environment, every news release or press announcement drives traffic to your client's website—so offering this service can be critical in making your clients' communications campaigns successful.
- A **video producer or production company** can become an important supplier, recording media announcements and editing them to create short programs

to post on your client's website, on YouTube, and in newsletters distributed by e-mail. If you don't want to make the significant investment in video editing software and additional monitors, make friends with a producer who can provide these services at a reasonable cost.

- Before long, you will find that you can troubleshoot your own computer system with relative ease—but if you're used to calling the IT department whenever something goes wrong, you will want to have the phone number of a **computer support expert** who can help keep your system up and running. Downtime is anathema to the self-employed: While your computer screen blinks a single question mark at you, you can't complete projects, get your e-mail, keep your records up to date, or any of the other services you depend on your system to provide.

- While printed pieces seem less prevalent with each passing year, it's still a good idea to have a favorite **commercial printer** to whom you can turn with a short-run digital project or a full-scale, thirty-two-page annual report. Look for one that can accept orders electronically through a unified workflow system, so you can place an order, upload the files to be printed, and sit back and wait for the sales or production representative to call you with questions and proofs.

- When you get a project that involves the kind of transcription, data, or production work that does not warrant your considerable expertise, you will be so glad for your connection with a **support person or service** that can take care of such things for you at a lower cost than your own billable rate. You can keep billing away at your rate while your temporary, contracted clerical assistant does the time-consuming busy work.

How do you find all of these services? Here are some resources that will help:

- **Professional associations.** Find the local chapters of organizations like the American Advertising Federation, the American Institute of Graphic Arts (AIGA), and the Graphic Arts Association for illustrators, artists, and designers. For website designers and developers, try the Web Design and Developers Association or the International Webmasters Association. The Digital Video Professionals Association and the Association of Video Professionals will lead you to videographers and production companies in your area.

- **Referrals.** When you attend networking events, or when you get together with friends in the business, ask the people you meet about suppliers they've used in their own work. You'll get the skinny about which suppliers are good, as well as which you may want to avoid.
- **Online reviews and resources.** There's no shortage of information online, so even if you have a good source for information about a particular supplier, run the name through your search engine and see what comes up. Not only will you find websites chock-full of samples and background about people you may be considering, but you may also uncover comments and facts that may help you shy away from problem suppliers.

From the Field

Anjani Webb, Debut Public Relations

"I keep learning—you cannot stop learning."

Would you hire a public relations firm led by a woman in her early 20s, who finished college just a couple of years ago?

Plenty of clients do exactly that, according to Anjani Webb, the owner of Debut Public Relations (www.debutpr.com). Webb runs her four-person agency virtually, as all three of her coworkers live in different states, from Washington, D.C., to Florida. "We signed two new clients recently, and I've had to turn others away," she said. "The big PR firms only care about national accounts—so that's where we come in. There's an entire sector of small businesses and nonprofits that haven't hired someone full-time with adequate experience. They're doing all these great things in their communities, but they don't know how to spread the word."

To ensure the success of its media relations and promotional efforts, Debut PR offers a strong website design service to its clients in addition to public relations planning. "I can come up with a great PR plan, but if the company doesn't have a great website, it can all fall flat," Webb said.

The brevity of Webb's career belies the depth of her experience. Right after high school, she held a paid internship in the Washington, D.C., office of Alaska senator Ted Stevens. "His speechwriter at the time was young, probably twenty-seven," Webb said, "and I thought it was very interesting that she had such a large role. I started asking questions, and he suggested I go into communications."

A few years later, while she studied at Liberty University in Lynchburg, Virginia, an internship for a freelance PR practitioner threw Webb headlong into the roles of copywriter, media relations specialist, and account manager. By the time she graduated from college, she knew she was ready to take on some significant responsibilities on behalf of a diverse group of clients.

"I got a few full-time jobs, and then someone approached me to do PR for her," she said. "She was opening the first frozen yogurt shop in the area, and I knew I could help her be successful. It grew from there."

Webb founded Debut PR in 2010, launching a website and making contact with potential clients—all while holding down a full-time job as development and marketing coordinator for the High Point, North Carolina, chapter of The Salvation Army. She's been married since 2009 to her business partner, Jace Webb, and runs her home office from a bedroom in her Morrisville, North Carolina, home. "I have nobody to blame but myself, but my business is my nights and weekends," she said. "I'm young and I'm adaptive, and I love it."

Turning her youth to her advantage is second nature to Webb and her three business cohorts. "I don't know what people did before the web, because of my age," she said. "Everything has changed so much. I've been lucky that I keep learning—you cannot stop learning. Today it's about Google Plus. A year and a half ago it was about Twitter. For some of these PR practitioners to feel above it all, that's going to leave them behind. That's our advantage: We are accessible, we are reachable, we are teachable."

To others considering a home-based PR business, Webb offers this advice: "Don't just focus on gaining relationships, but make them good relationships. I have been wildly successful with reporters because they say I'm one of the only ones who care! For me, that's super-simple. I'm not faking it; I really care about these people."

Keeping Things Honest: A General Business Agreement

When you begin working with a supplier, it's wise to put some general information down in writing to be sure you share a mutual understanding about your working relationship. This need not be a major contract drawn up by your attorney, but it does need to cover the parameters of the project(s) you plan to do together, and how the money will be distributed between you and your supplier.

Put together a letter of agreement that details the following:

- The name of the client or clients you and your supplier will serve
- The kinds of services your supplier will provide to you for this job
- The way you will pay the supplier, and the terms of this payment (i.e., net thirty days from receipt of invoice, or another method as you prefer)
- The expected time frame of this assignment
- The final deliverables you will receive from your supplier
- The procedure for early termination of this agreement, should there be a dispute
- How conflicts between the partners will be resolved (i.e., through outside mediation or another means)
- Your responsibility to pay (or not) should the client not pay you on time, or if the client is dissatisfied with the work and refuses to pay

Once you have a letter with which you and your supplier both feel comfortable, make two copies so you can each have a signed original copy of the letter. Both of you will sign each copy (two signatures per copy).

If this seems like a lot of rigmarole for your new, bureaucracy-free way of working in your home office, consider this: What will you do if your client loves your writing, but hates the brochure design your selected graphic artist creates? Are you still required to pay the artist, even though the client won't pay you for the design she hates? What if the client and the artist just plain don't get along, and the client wants him off the job? Settle these issues in advance in good faith, and you can bring these conflicts to a swift, equitable conclusion.

The Vendor Non-Competition Agreement

Within your letter of agreement with your supplier, you may wish to include a clause that keeps this supplier from soliciting your clients for a set period after the term of your agreement ends.

Non-competition agreements between an agency and a supplier may or may not be enforceable, depending on your state and the way your agreement is written. Generally, the suppliers you bring into a client assignment will not have your public relations skills, so they may be no real threat to you should they approach your client directly for continued business.

In today's ultra-competitive marketplace, however, you may see the possibility that a graphic artist could team with another PR professional, or that a website developer could turn around and offer social networking services that you offer as well. To ease your own mind, a non-competition clause in your letter of agreement may be the practical choice.

To be enforceable, the non-compete agreement must have certain components:

1. It must demonstrate that a non-competition agreement is required to protect your interests, i.e., if the supplier somehow could damage your reputation with your client by working with her directly. (This is a tough one to prove, should the situation ever arise.)
2. It must have a defined time frame: a year or eighteen months are considered reasonable. You cannot forbid the supplier from working with your client forever.
3. It must specify that your supplier has become privy to trade secrets or confidential information about the client that he could use to compete against you.

Your non-competition clause may have all of these elements and still not be enforceable in a court of law, but simply signing the agreement may be enough to keep most suppliers from soliciting your clients after the initial assignment ends.

Confidentiality Agreements

If your work connects you with major corporations, well-known retail brands, or individuals with highly visible lives, you may be asked to sign a confidentiality agreement before these lucrative clients allow you to learn much about them.

This is fairly standard procedure with high-profile clients, especially if you will be introducing proprietary technology or working closely with research and development teams. Your promise not to share information with the media, the competition, or anyone who might have even casual contact with competitors is vital to the nature of your business.

The confidentiality agreement (also called a nondisclosure agreement) stipulates that you understand that confidential information has monetary value, you know that disclosing this information could do considerable harm to your client, and you will not "deliver or disclose" such information unless you are authorized in writing by your client to do so. It may contain a great deal of legal language, but basically, this is the gist of what you may be asked to sign.

Even a confidentiality agreement has a time limit: Once the information becomes part of the public domain—i.e., once your client releases it to the media or announces it to customers—you are no longer held to the promise of confidentiality.

Should you sign? The facts are clear: The client has a right to maintain its confidentiality, and you won't get the job if you're unwilling to agree to nondisclosure. If you're truly uneasy about the language in the agreement, pass it by your lawyer before you sign it.

Your Graphic Identity

Now that you have a name, a formal business structure, an address, and a phone number, it's time to start working on your graphic identity—a logo that will be consistent throughout all of your hard copy and electronic marketing materials.

As a home-based business, your company needs these materials in place before you begin any active marketing. A logo gives your business a look of stability, as if you have been in business for some time and you have taken the time to develop your professional image. At the same time, it provides that all-important first impression, making a visual statement about who you are and what kind of company you run. The logo signifies your brand, the kind of professional persona you want to present to the world, and the promise of value that you make to your clients.

Such an important element of your new business requires some thought about what you want your business to be. Go back to your business plan and read what you wrote about your mission and goals. How do these statements become a value proposition to your potential clients? Conveying this proposition graphically can be a challenge, but if you work with a smart graphic designer who can extract the heart of this message and turn it into an evocative design, you will see the result as it emerges from the process.

What goes into a strong logo?

- **Make it readable.** If you go with an all-type logo that states your business name in an attractive way, resist the urge to juggle or stack the letters, or to add so many frills that your clients have to squint to figure out what it says.

- **Make it memorable.** A single, strong graphic can say much more than a lot of representational images, and it will stay in the minds of your audience.
- **Make it meaningful.** If you've given your company an obscure name, use the logo to explain it. If you plan to pursue a specific specialty, your logo might include an element that links you visually with that field.
- **Make it different.** Your logo should illustrate the uniqueness of your business, not your efforts to be just like someone else's business.

Once you've got a logo, your artist (or you, if you have this skill) can create company stationery, envelopes, and business cards. It's up to you if you need to actually print these materials, or if you simply create electronic templates that you can use in Microsoft Word, Apple Pages, or whatever word processing software you've chosen. You may be able to eliminate the expense of a print run by choosing the print-on-demand option, as most inkjet or laser printers will print a high-quality image on stationery-quality papers.

Be sure to get a high-resolution (300 dpi) JPEG file of your logo from your designer, so you can use this logo on your website, as part of the signature for your e-mails, on your Facebook page, and in all the other formats in which you promote your business.

Sample Logo

Your Business Card

What information should be on your business card? What you do and don't include may be a matter of personal preference, but here's a good rule of thumb:

- Your business name and logo
- Your name
- Your title—whatever you've chosen to call yourself, based on your status as a sole proprietor, partnership, or corporation
- Your mailing address
- Your business telephone number
- Your mobile phone number if it's different from your business number
- Your Skype name
- Your e-mail address
- Your website address
- If you have room (or on the back), any online sites beyond your website through which your clients can reach you. These may include your Facebook, Google Plus, Twitter, and LinkedIn names, your Tumblr or WordPress blog site, or your online profile on a site in your area of specialization.

If this seems like a lot of information to put on a little card . . . it is. How much you include depends on how connected you want or need to appear. If your clients do not require or won't fully appreciate your extensive knowledge and use of the online world, you may opt to list all of these links on your website, and simply direct your clients to that site for all of your additional information.

Your Online Identity

You've got a logo, you've got a business plan that details your company's purpose and goals, you know what kinds of clients you want to pursue, and you know what services you can offer these clients. It's time to tell the world about your new business, and the fastest, most far-reaching, and most comprehensive way to do this is with a website.

Your Domain Name

Keep it simple! The best domain name for your business website is the name of your business. Clients and prospects will have no trouble finding you with this, even if they just take a guess. Even more important, search engines will find you quickly if prospects come looking for you through Google or Bing.

You can register your domain name through any one of the hundreds of website hosting services. When you register, you need to specify where your domain will live, so it makes sense to do the registration through the hosting service you've chosen. GoDaddy, Hosting.com, Network Solutions, Register.com, Verio.com, Domain.com, and Yahoo! are just a few of the well-known services that offer both domain name registration and web hosting service. Some of these will register your domain name for free when you enter into an annual contract with them for web hosting.

Build Your Website

It's your online brochure and your sales force that never sleeps—your website will become your most valuable tool in attracting new business. Even if you're still yearning for that manual typewriter on which you wrote your first high school term paper, you need to build a website, keep it online and active, and update it regularly if you want to be in business in the twenty-first century.

Happily, it's never been easier to do this, as you no longer need to write complex code or have superior graphic design skills to build your own site. Simple applications like Apple's iWeb and Microsoft's WebMatrix, online web building sites like Moonfruit, iBuilt, Intuit's Homestead, and many others, and tools offered by your selected domain hosting service all make the process reasonably simple.

Debug: Flash or No Flash?

Do you need an animated opening sequence and lots of moving graphics on your website? If you do, make sure you include them using web-based software with open architecture if you want Apple iPhone and iPad users to view your site. Many of the animated graphics on websites are designed using Adobe Flash Builder, and as of this writing, Flash doesn't run on the iPhone and iPad. Apple made the choice to exclude compatibility with the proprietary Flash program from its mobile products in favor of HTML5, H.264, CSS, and JavaScript, web standards that are open to anyone to use. If you're adding video, audio, or animation to your website, choose a website building package that uses these open programs.

What should you include in your website? Your site can be as simple or as elaborate as you like, as long as it provides the information your visitors came there to find. Generally, your prospects arrive with these questions about you:

- **Does this company specialize in what I need?** Explain your company's focus and areas of specialization on the first page. Don't waste your visitors' time with extraneous information and fancy graphics if, in the end, you don't provide the services they require.
- **Who runs this company?** An "About Us" page with your professional biography, a photo of you, and your unique skills will help prospects get to know you and decide if they want to contact you.
- **What services does this company provide?** A "Services" page with descriptions of the kinds of things you do for clients will attract the clients who are right for you.
- **Who are this company's current and former clients?** Some business owners worry that if they list their clients on a website, competitors will see the list and cherry-pick the clients they want to steal. Here's my take on this: If your relationship with these clients is so tenuous that a competitor could make a phone call and take them away from you, they weren't really yours in the first place. Go ahead and show off your client list to the world. Prospects want to see that you've worked with clients who are of similar size and scope to their own companies. This solidifies their impression of your capabilities.
- **Can I see some samples of this company's work?** A page of your triumphs can be very effective, especially if a project generated lots of coverage or if you have plenty of colorful, exciting-looking communications campaign pieces to showcase. Provide a short paragraph about each project to emphasize the extent of your services and the height of your triumph.
- **How do I contact this company?** Now that you've hooked them in, make sure your prospects can get in touch with you in the way they prefer. There's nothing more frustrating to a potential client than clicking "Contact Us" and finding a little form they have to fill out to send a message to an invisible e-mail address. Give your prospects your phone number(s), e-mail address, Facebook name, Twitter name, LinkedIn profile name, Skype name, and any other handles you may have to make yourself as easy as possible to reach.

Thinkpoint: Making Yourself Findable Online

Search engine optimization (SEO) sounds like a scary process that only super-geeks and web gurus understand, but you can perform some basic optimization within your website on your own to make sure that the right searches lead to your site.

First, sign your site up for Google Analytics. This nifty tool tracks all the visits your site gets on a daily basis, and what search words they use to find you. (Your website hosting service may provide a set of tools that do this as well.) You can see at a glance which terms bring people to your site—and which do not. Now you can build the right search terms into the headlines on your site, to maximize the possibility that your site will pop up into the top of the search results.

If you want people to find you when they search on "distilled spirits public relations," for example, plug this phrase into your site's headline and the first paragraph of your copy. Make your headline, "Public relations services specializing in distilled spirits and other alcoholic beverages," and use these words again in your body copy. Keep using them on every relevant page on your website.

It may take three weeks or more before search engines lead prospects directly to your site. Track this by searching on your desired terms on Google and Bing. Keep in mind that if your desired search terms are too general—if, for example, your terms are "computer technology public relations"—there may be many other companies that will rise above you in the search results. The more specific you can be in your selling proposition, the better your chances of rising to the top of the list.

If you answer these questions for prospects who visit your website, they have what they need to make an informed decision about contacting you directly. Best of all, they have this whether they're surfing for a new PR firm at 3:00 a.m. or changing planes in London's Heathrow Airport on the way to a trade show in Munich.

Announcing Your New Business

Are you ready to make some noise?

It's time to do what we do best: Alert the public that there's a new business in town. Of all the things you've had to do to start your business, this is the one that comes the most naturally.

With so many avenues for your announcement, you can make the most of the opportunity to draw early attention to your new enterprise.

- Send out a news release and a professional head-and-shoulders photo of yourself to your local business media, and to the trade magazines and websites in your market niches. Tailor this release to each target market, so there's no question about its relevance in each case.
- Follow up with editors to renew old contacts and establish new relationships. If you're approaching new editors with whom you have not worked before, it's a great idea to call just to introduce yourself. This will make the next call—for a story pitch—just that much easier.
- Post your opening day announcement to your Facebook and LinkedIn pages (see chapter 10), and tweet about it on Twitter.
- Send links to stories about your new business to your list of professional and personal contacts. In the e-mail, ask for business! Explain your business focus, and request referrals for potential new business from friends, associates, and former clients.
- If you've started a blog on your website or on a remote site, your first day in business is definitely something to blog about. Post links to this blog on LinkedIn and Facebook as well.
- If your business base will be primarily local, hold an open house event. Show off your home office (your work-at-home status will make many people envious), serve sweets and business-appropriate beverages, and send each guest home with a small gift (a little box of mints, nuts, or chocolates works well here) and a card printed with your logo and contact information.
- If your initial budget allows for it, send out a printed piece with a cover letter to reintroduce yourself to professional contacts you have known. Include your photo in the body of the letter, to remind them of their connection with you. The printed piece need not be elaborate—you can direct recipients to your website for in-depth information—but it should be striking enough to make your prospects stop and look at it.

You're on your way! It's time to cross over the communications line and start marketing yourself and your company's services. We'll cover this in depth in the next chapter, and in chapter 10.

06

Money: How to Make It

When you're in business for yourself, you have two full-time jobs: (1) Developing and completing the work for current clients; and (2) Attracting new clients.

In the earliest days of your new company, attracting new clients becomes your first priority. As your client list grows and you have all the work you can handle, it's easy to assume that you don't really need to market your business to new clients, at least in the short term. This may be the most dangerous fallacy for the self-employed, however. Even when you have plenty of business on your desk, cultivating new client relationships needs to continue. Any business owner can tell you the story of a stable client base that suddenly dissolves because of a change in the economy, a new technology that makes a client's products obsolete, the sale of a client's company, or just plain bad business planning that forces a client to give up his public relations initiatives.

Let's start working on that initial client list, and a plan that will keep you on the lookout for new clients without taxing your time and energy to the maximum.

Who Will Hire You?

Your soon-to-be clients are out there, and chances are good that you already know them personally. If you've been working in PR for some time before launching your own business, you have contacts who know your capabilities and your reputation in your community or market. Even if you've never done client services because you handled internal PR for a corporation or nonprofit organization, you have colleagues and acquaintances with whom you networked in the past. It's time to bring all of those names together in one place, and to prioritize them in a three-tiered list. See the worksheet on the opposite page.

First, get a pad of lined paper.

1. Do a mind dump: Write down the names of everyone you know in the business community you plan to serve. This will probably be a fairly long list. Don't be choosy about what names to list; just get as many names as possible on paper.

2. Now go back through the list, and on a separate sheet (or sheets) of paper, write down the names of everyone on the list who cannot make a hiring decision about communications services. This is your "C" list. The people on this list may be able to suggest people you could contact for business, but they cannot actually hire you themselves. Cross these names off of your mind-dump list as you move them to the C list.

3. With all of your C-listers crossed off, your mind-dump list is a little shorter. Go through it again, and on a clean sheet of paper, write down all the people whom you do not know well, but who probably are familiar with your name and professional skills—and who can also make the decision about hiring a freelance PR firm. The people on this list will be interested to hear that you now work for yourself. They may already be served by another freelance PR person or a larger agency, but you see them at networking events and you know them well enough to chat with them there. This group is your "B" list. Cross these names off your mind-dump list as you move them to the B list.

4. Who's left? The remaining names should be people you know well. These people can make decisions about hiring a PR professional, and they have a high opinion of you and your work. They may be former clients or coworkers of your clients, people with whom you've served on nonprofit boards, people you've met repeatedly at networking events, friends in the industry, even editors and producers who could refer you to people they know within your target industries. This is your "A" list, the people you can contact today with confidence, knowing that they will take your call and meet with you to discuss your current capabilities.

5. Start working with your A list, gathering their contact information and preparing your approach to them. (We'll talk more about this in chapter 10.)

Now that you've completed your three-tiered list, how long is your A list? Unless you're very new to the industry, chances are good that you have between twenty and thirty names on it, and maybe more. This is an excellent starting number for your direct marketing efforts, a manageable list of prospects that will not overwhelm you as you begin to solicit them for business.

As you add clients to your roster and complete projects for them that demonstrate your ability to serve them well, broaden your marketing efforts to include people on your B list. Your A list prospects know you professionally or personally, so they don't necessarily require a major capabilities presentation to see that you can handle their work. Your B list, however, contains people who only know your skills secondhand, and only have a casual relationship with you. It will take more work to approach these people and convince them that you have the skills they need, and they may expect more evidence of your new company's stability before they consider hiring you. A portfolio full of work samples will help you make a compelling case.

The Right Number of Clients

How many clients do you actually need? This depends on you: your ability to balance the workload for a range of clients, the amount of money you need to make each week, your fees, and the goals you itemized in your business plan.

Companies of all sizes look at their customer base using this simple rule: **80 percent of your business comes from 20 percent of your customers.** The 80/20 rule works like this: If you have ten clients and you make $100,000 per year, two of these clients (20 percent of your base) will provide $80,000 (80 percent) of your income. These are your anchor clients, the ones that keep the doors of your business open. The other eight clients fill in the last $20,000. The numbers may fluctuate slightly from one company to the next, but this rule of thumb tends to hold true across markets, industries, and continents.

With just 20 percent of your clients providing the vast majority of your income, you can see the danger in assuming that once you've engaged these two big clients, you can stop prospecting for new business. The day will come—and it always comes—when something will change with one of these two mainstay clients. Maybe the company will be sold to a large conglomerate with its own in-house PR team. Maybe the economy will go sour and the client will pull all of its business in-house, ending its relationships with all of its outside suppliers. Maybe your wonderful client will retire, and the new person hired by the company will bring in his own favorite

PR firm. Maybe your brilliant PR work cannot save this client from its own inevitable demise, for reasons that have nothing at all to do with you. Or maybe you will make an error that will cause the client to discontinue your services. All kinds of things can happen, most of them completely out of your control—but the result is the same: Suddenly you've lost as much as 40 percent of your income.

The moral of this story: Never, ever bank on a single client, no matter how solid and dependable that client may seem.

This may mean that you find yourself maintaining a larger client list as a safeguard against this inevitable attrition. My rule of thumb on this: Always have one more client than you feel you need. If serving the additional client means that you work a few extra hours a week or the occasional Saturday, so be it. Smaller clients can grow to be larger, creating the cushion you need to survive the blow when one of your anchor clients no longer requires your services.

What to Charge

If you bought this book, opened to the index and skipped directly to here, welcome! When I've answered your questions about what to charge, please take the time to read the rest of the book—you will find plenty of other useful advice that will help you build and maintain a successful public relations business.

Public relations agencies charge their clients by the hour, with different fees based on the job each person on the team actually performs. Top practitioners—account supervisors, consultants, senior copywriters, art directors, and the like—charge the highest hourly rates, while graphic artists, account executives, and support staff usually have lower rates. (If a creative director is involved, the rates can skyrocket.)

Rates also differ by market. Agencies in New York City, Los Angeles, Dallas, Chicago, Atlanta, Miami, and other big cities are considerably more expensive than those of us in smaller cities like Madison, Wisconsin; Rochester, New York; Reno, Nevada; or Greensboro, North Carolina. In addition, rates often are determined by level of experience: If you're just starting out in the PR business, your clients may not be willing to pay the high fees they would pay for someone with thirty years of client service and accumulated expertise.

So, how do you determine what you can charge?

First, find out what agencies in your area charge by the hour for their services. If you don't come from an agency background yourself, talk to some of your contacts who do, or those who hire agencies for their work. Remember that you're the head of your own company now, so think of yourself in the same terms as the top people at other agencies.

When you have rates that you can compare from several agencies, calculate the average of the top rates. This, more or less, is the going rate for expert public relations services.

Now, knock 20 percent off that. Give yourself the competitive advantage of being slightly less expensive than the top people at the bigger agencies. Your future clients expect to pay for your services, but they don't expect to pay a solo practitioner what they would pay for a big agency with a lot of overhead.

Approach your clients with a fee that represents your qualifications—a fee that gives you credibility. If you charge too much, your clients may not see any advantage to hiring you over the larger agencies with their extensive resources. Charge too little, and your clients will think you don't have faith in your own qualifications, which will lead them to believe that your services may not have real value.

Get Used to Talking about Money

I once sat down with a young copywriter who had just gone into business for herself. I interviewed her because I had some overflow writing I thought she could handle quite well, based on her writing samples and her experience. We were having a grand time in this meeting until I asked her about her billable rate. All of a sudden, she cast her eyes downward and shuffled her feet under the table, and uttered only a string of "ums" and "ers." I finally said, "For heaven's sake, do you charge $200 an hour or something?"

She looked up in surprise. "No," she said, "I'm $26 an hour."

"Then why are you so hesitant to say so?" I asked.

She had no real answer to this, except that she did not like to talk about money. The fact that her rate was so low and she seemed embarrassed to discuss payment at all, even though it was clear that she would expect to be paid for her work, cast doubts on her ability to succeed as a freelancer. Indeed, just a few months later, she took a full-time job in a corporate communications setting.

If you empathize with this young woman's discomfort, it's time to overcome your fears of discussing your rates with potential clients. They know that you expect to be paid, and they need information about how much and in what kind of time frame to help them make the decision to hire you. It's up to you to provide clear, direct answers with no hint of self-deprecation, so they know that you are a serious professional with high business standards for above-board communication with your clients.

When a client asks, "What are your rates?" answer them smoothly and succinctly with, "My rate is $100 an hour. I can invoice you on a weekly or monthly basis, as you prefer, and payment is due in thirty days."

There, that wasn't so hard, was it? Next, resist the urge to drop your rate precipitously if the potential client balks at the rate. As soon as you say, "Well, I could charge you $65 an hour instead," you've blown your credibility—and the client will believe that no matter what he pays you, it's going to be too much, because you're so quick to try to renegotiate. Stick to your guns, with the understanding that not every client is the right one for you.

Structuring Your Fees

Once you've determined your base rate, you may want to create a scale of fees to accommodate different kinds of clients. You're not required to do this, but it may help you gain business if you need to reach beyond your target market sectors to fill your client roster during tough economic times.

Your **corporate rate** is the rate you charge your larger business clients. This is your base rate; any discounts you make to other kinds of clients start with this one.

Your **nonprofit rate** may be 10 to 20 percent below your corporate rate. It's a nominal fee change that may have little effect on your income in general, but it will be meaningful to nonprofit organizations that expect to pay less than you would charge big corporations.

Your **subcontractor rate** takes into account that the agency or company to which you contract your services will mark up your rate before billing their client. For example, let's say an agency comes to you to take on their overflow news release writing in advance of a major trade show, because of your expertise in a specialized field. This agency expects to make some profit on the work you do, so they will mark up your rate 15–20 percent when they bill it to the client. To do this, they must be sure that your rate is not higher than the rate they already charge their client for copywriting services. Any concession you are willing to make on your rate to them will make them more likely to come to you again when they hit their next time crunch. You still make a good amount on the work you do for them, and they still make a little money on that work as well. (Some agencies will tell you what they are willing to pay, i.e., "We pay our freelancers $65 per hour." If the rate they quote you is less than you intended to charge, tell them so. They need your expertise, and they may be willing to make an exception to work with you.)

Debug: The Pay-For-Placement Model

If you're fairly new to the PR industry, you may be tempted to charge clients by the media placement instead of by the hour, as an incentive for clients to give your services a try. Pay-for-placement is attractive to inexperienced clients, because it appears to lower the risk of them paying for a great deal of agency effort with limited gain in actual media coverage.

In reality, this arrangement can cause many more problems than it solves. For one, your client is paying only for placements, so there's no money for strategy development or crafting of the message. The client has forfeited the benefit of your expertise, leaving you to do nothing but dial and e-mail to get stories in print.

You will invest the aforementioned great deal of time, but it can be very difficult to collect on that investment. Imagine, for example, that you've set a per-placement price with a client of $100 per website placement, and $300 for each newspaper, radio, or television placement. (These are absurdly small amounts, meant only as examples.) You've written a news release or a pitch, gone through several rounds of edits and changes with your client, sent the release and then followed up with editors to engage their interest and encourage coverage . . . and you receive a couple of placements on websites and in a daily newspaper or two. By now you've invested many hours, but the client is not paying you for your time—he's paying for the placements. You can't possibly recoup the cost of your time.

Alternately, you may make a deal with the client that he will pay for all of your time when you secure one or more of the placements he wants. When you get the story in the *Wall Street Journal* or the *New York Times,* you hand your client an invoice for thousands of dollars. You can hear the response: "That much for one placement?"

Worse, as you don't have control of the media's treatment of your client's news, editors who pick up the story may position it in a way that makes the client unhappy. The client may decide that he should not pay for that placement at all—and that you should contact the media and somehow "make it right" for free. Now what do you do?

Pay-for-placement may bring you a few early clients, but you're virtually guaranteed to find it an untenable arrangement.

Other Billable Items

In addition to your time, you can charge clients for use of reference materials for which you probably paid some significant fees.

- When you build a media list using one of the online tools (Cision, Vocus, or PR Web, for example), use of these pricey tools is a legitimate, billable business expense. It's unlikely that you can bill one client for the entire annual price of the service, but you can break it down over a series of clients who need media lists.
- If you use a manual or electronic clipping service to search through publications to find mentions of your client's company, bill the fees for this to your client.
- Any time you post a news release on PR Newswire or PR Web, remember to charge your client the fee you are charged for these services.
- A portion of your subscription to ProfNet or another fee-based service for reporter leads can be billed to a client when a lead results in an inquiry (not necessarily a placement) on the client's behalf.
- Postage, packing, and shipping fees are all billable (though it's unwise to nickel-and-dime your client over postage that's less than $10).
- Large amounts of office supplies required for a single project are legitimate expenses.
- Of course, any subcontracted services should be billed to your client in your regular invoice. You can mark up these services (that is, charge an additional percentage for your management of the project) at a rate of 18 to 20 percent above the amount your vendor billed to you. These are fairly standard markup rates in the industry, although larger agencies often apply higher markups.
- Commercial printing, CD or DVD duplication, or any other production services are billable—also with an 18 to 20 percent markup.

Making Your "Nut"

How much money do you need to make?

The answer from your gut may be, "As much as I can," but it's good to know what you actually need so you can tell when your business is operating successfully. With this information, you will know when you have succeeded in supporting yourself and, if necessary, your household with your business.

The total amount of money you need in an average month—the amount I call the "nut"—may be larger than you think. It's worth computing this number to be sure you're billing enough time each month to actually cover your expenses, fuel your savings, and help you build a cushion for less prosperous times.

Calculating the Nut

List the amount you pay **per month** for each of the items below.

Rent/mortgage	_____
Utilities (gas, electric, water)	_____
Telephone (landline)	_____
Mobile phone	_____
Cable service	_____
Internet service	_____
Car payment	_____
Gas	_____
Car maintenance	_____
Groceries	_____
Eating out	_____
Home repairs	_____
Cleaning/grounds services	_____
Prescriptions	_____
Health insurance	_____
Life insurance	_____
Disability insurance	_____
Clothing	_____
Hair/makeup/manicure	_____
Health club	_____
School fees/tuition	_____
Credit card debt	_____
Other expenses	_____
Savings per month	_____

TOTAL _____

Percentage of total nut to come from PR business* _____

Multiply the Total by this percentage in decimal terms (i.e., 50 percent = .50)

TOTAL PR Business Nut per month _____

Divide this by 4 weeks/month _____

This is what your business must earn per week.

Now, divide this amount by the rate you plan to charge per hour. _____

This is the number of hours you must bill per week to make your nut. _____

* If you share household expenses with a spouse, significant other or roommate, calculate the percentage you are expected to provide.

Now you know how many hours you need to work and bill each week to cover your household and business expenses. Many sole practitioners discover that they need to work and bill fewer hours than they originally expected. This is good—it means that if you have enough business and work a little harder, you can begin to see a profit in fairly short order.

If you are in the group who find that they must work many more hours than they realized to make the nut, however, I advise you to reassess your household expenses before you cut the cord from your full-time job. Use this time to pay off consumer debt, trim your entertainment budget, and build a cash reserve to tide you over if it takes a few months before your business begins to pay you regularly. Even if you have clients from your very first day as a sole practitioner, it can take several weeks or months before you complete your first projects and invoice your clients—and then thirty days or more before the checks arrive. We'll talk about how to manage client payment terms in the "How to Get Paid" section, which is coming up in a moment.

Making a Profit

How much money do you want to make? Most of us would rather make more than we do now, and we could do so with the time we have available. When you work for yourself and work alone, however, it's easy to place roadblocks between yourself and your earning ability. Here are some watch-outs to help you stay on track during the workday.

1. **Turn off the TV.** Unless you're monitoring the news to see a story you've placed about one of your clients, there's no reason to have the television on while you're working. It's basic human reflex to look at whatever is moving in the room, so don't create that temptation.

2. **Turn off your e-mail.** Close your e-mail program when you're writing, so you're not distracted every few minutes by the sound of new messages arriving. You can't bill the time you spend looking at someone's cute kitty pictures or deleting spam.

3. **Limit your pro bono projects.** For reasons that seem nonsensical once you're running your at-home business, nonprofit organizations often believe that since we work from home and "on our own schedule," we have oodles of time to give away writing their newsletters, promoting their events, and volunteering on-site. It's great to feel passionate about a cause, but you can't eat passion. Be realistic about how many committees you can run and how much

time you can invest in someone's non-paying work. You are well within your rights to say, "Gee, I already have a major pro bono project this year, so I'll have to pass on the one you're offering. I can recommend some great people to help you, though."

4. **Track your time.** We'll talk more about this in a moment, but time tracking proves to be the best way to get your full value out of every project.

5. **Streamline your management time.** You can't bill the time you spend managing your company, so use the many tools available to you to expedite your recordkeeping, filing, invoicing, bill paying and other administrative tasks. Invest in good financial management software (like QuickBooks Pro or Peachtree), and scan handwritten documents to file on your hard drive to eliminate piles of papers that must be filed in manila folders. Some tasks turn out to be unavoidable—like preparing your records for your accountant at tax time—but they need not compromise your billable time for hours on end.

Getting Your Full Value with Time Tracking

How can you be sure you're billing clients for all the time you spend on their projects? The only surefire way is to track your time. Time tracking involves recording everything you do each day, and how long each task took to perform.

If you come from a public relations agency background, you're already in the habit of tracking your time by hand in your desk calendar or on a notepad, or on the agency's time tracking computer software. For people who have always worked in a corporate or nonprofit situation and received a salary, however, keeping track of every task and how long it took may seem like a daunting responsibility.

Let me assure you that time tracking becomes second nature very quickly. First, when you add up the hours it took to complete a client project, you may be amazed at how much time you actually invested—all of which you can now bill to the client. And second, when you begin to see checks arrive in payment for your invoices, your motivation to keep excellent time records will increase exponentially.

You can track your time quickly, immediately, and efficiently by using the time entry screen in any one of many small business financial management software packages, like QuickBooks Pro, OpenAir, Cashboard, TimeLog or many others. These programs allow you to record any time interval you choose—from one minute to up to twenty-four hours in a day—and then transfer that time directly into a client's invoice, complete with notes about what you did during each time interval.

Each software brand has its own functionality, of course, but here's what a basic time entry chart looks like.

Job	Service item	Notes	M	Tu	W	Th	F	Sa	Su	Total
Acme news release	Copy-writing	Write news release		1.25	1					2.25
Smith Co. social net-working campaign	Blog/Post	Write and post blog about green energy, post links to it from Face-book and Twitter		2.30						2.30

Time gets entered in decimal places that represent hours and fractions of an hour (so 2.30 = 2 hours, 18 minutes).

The sooner you get into the habit of recording your time at the completion of each task, the more money you will make more quickly. It's easy to forget that you made six phone calls for a client spread out during the course of a day, but when you add up these six five-minute calls, you suddenly have an entire half-hour to bill to the client. If you're away from your computer, jot down the time in your notebook to record later.

Profit Booster

Some time tracking software applications allow you to keep a small window open on your desktop all the time, to remind you to record your time as soon as you come to the end of a task, or whenever you're interrupted by a phone call or a client meeting. Having this visual reminder on your screen all the time can help you remember to track your hours.

Track Your Expenses

If you take on expenses on behalf of your client for printing, postage, purchase of special materials like fancy presentation folders, or posting a news release to a pay-per-post online news service (like PRWeb or PR Newswire), make sure you actually bill your client for these services. There's nothing worse than discovering months after the fact that you forgot to include an expense in your final project invoice. Not only is this an embarrassing situation, but your client will not think highly of the additional expense after she closed out her budget for that project.

Most financial software packages allow you to link these expenses with the project to which they apply, so you can bring these figures into the client invoice with a single click. For this to work, of course, you need to enter all of the expenses into your financial software, so they are ready to appear when you need them.

This may require you to shake down your suppliers for their invoices, so you have a full reckoning of all the expenses when you are ready to bill the client. Make delivery of their final invoice a requirement in your letter of agreement with them, so they have some obligation to bill you promptly. If you're working with small shops like your own, the owner may be doing the weekly invoicing and may be just as reticent to spend his time on non-billable administrative tasks as you are. Don't be afraid to pick up the phone and call your supplier to request the invoice. He wants to be paid, just as you do, and he will appreciate your eagerness to get him his money.

How to Get Paid

Many years ago, my employer at the agency said to me, "You know, I just love this work so much I would do it for free. It's a good thing someone else is in charge of the finances, or I'd forget to even bill the client for the work."

How wonderful for her that her work satisfied her so completely! Honestly, many of us feel this way about working with clients, solving their problems, filling critical needs in their business lives, and celebrating their successes. This satisfaction plays an important role in our daily motivation. That's why we work from home businesses of our own—to have this kind of day-to-day interaction with clients, and to do work that we enjoy this much.

No matter how much we love the work, however, the world gives us a stone-cold dose of reality when the mortgage is due and our bank accounts don't contain enough cash to cover it. We need to get paid regularly and promptly.

Here, in a nutshell, is a step-by-step guide to making sure each project ends in a nice check from a happy client.

Set Your Client's Expectations from the Outset

Prepare a written estimate of the time it will take you to complete the project, and have your client sign it to indicate his approval of the project budget. Even for small projects, it pays to have this sheet of paper that signifies agreement that you will be paid for the work, and how much. (We'll talk more about estimating later in this chapter.) It can be tough to wait to begin a project until you receive this signed document, but any work you do before the signature arrives is truly at your own risk. The client may reconsider the project based on your estimate, so you will not be paid for unauthorized work

Set Payment Terms

At the end of your estimate, describe the way you expect to be paid. Most payments are expected in thirty days from the date of the invoice, and most clients expect to pay within thirty days. If you work for large corporations, there may be standardized payment schedules in place that a one-person company will not be able to alter, so be prepared to wait forty-five or even sixty days for your payment.

For very large, long-term projects, you are well within your rights to set terms that require payment at various stages of the project, including a down payment at the beginning. For example, let's say you're beginning a six-month product announcement project that will pay you a total of $30,000. Break this payment into three chunks: one-third ($10,000) at the beginning, to pay for your up-front expenses and investment of time; one-third when you deliver all the copy and design for the media kit and printed pieces to the client for review before production; and the final third at the end of the launch, when you deliver your report on the media placements and coverage you secured. This gives you the working capital you need to pay suppliers, while you support yourself during a time-consuming project.

Bill Ongoing Projects Every Month

Let's say a company hires you to handle ongoing, year-round media relations for the company. There's no end date, so you'll need to be paid regularly to keep up with all the time you accumulate. Bill the client every month on the last day of the month for whatever time you spent on their work during that month, with terms that require that you be paid thirty days after the date of the invoice. You can look forward to regular payments that allow you to manage your own finances with some confidence in the next check's arrival.

This can be equally useful for projects that do have a hard end date—like a new store opening or a product launch—but will take many months or even years to plan and execute. You can't wait until the end to be paid, so arrange with the client that you will send an invoice each month for payment within thirty days. It's up to you to watch the budget to be sure you don't use it up too early in the process, before the labor-intensive last few weeks kick you into high gear.

Bill Short Projects on Completion

Your clients will thank you for a prompt invoice at the end of a short project, within a day or two of completion, so they can get you paid and record the final total in their annual budgets. Delaying your invoice will only frustrate your client and make you appear to be less of a professional than your work demonstrated that you are.

The Lowdown on Retainers

It sounds like a great idea—and in most cases, it is a great idea to enter into a retainer agreement with clients. A retainer agreement states that you will be paid a set amount every month for the length of the retainer (usually a year), based on the level of activity you and your client estimate will be required from you through the course of the year. At the end of the year, you and your client re-estimate the amount of time required for the following year, and renew the retainer at this new amount per month.

Regular payments, predictable income, ongoing work . . . what could be bad about that? In the best situations, nothing goes wrong. It's more common, however, for plans to change, making either the client or the PR practitioner feel that the retainer agreement takes advantage of their good nature. Either the client demands far more work than the retainer covers, leaving the PR person feeling like she's not getting the full value for her work; or the client's workload turns out to be significantly smaller than projected, making the retainer payment seem like an enormous rip-off for the value the client receives.

I had a client who insisted on a retainer, because he wanted the convenience of knowing exactly how much to pay me every month. Before six months went by, however, I found I was spending only a third of the time that we had predicted on his business. This meant that for every hour I spent on his work, I would bank two against the retainer.

After six months, I contacted him and said that we needed to reassess the amount, for which he was very grateful. However, before I could start billing him a lower retainer amount, I felt honor-bound to work off the extra time for which he had paid me. It took nearly a year to do this, so I found myself racking up hours every month for which I had been prepaid, but for which the money was long gone. This wrought havoc with my cash flow, but I kept a good client I might have lost if I had not been so vigilant about our agreement. We now have eschewed the retainer in favor of monthly invoices for the actual hours worked.

Retainers can be tricky, but if you make a point of monitoring the hours you spend on the client's work, and keep the lines of communication open between you and your client, you can make sure that your retainer works to your mutual advantage.

Charge Interest for Late Payments

If a client's account falls into arrears, you are completely right to attach a penalty to the amount in the form of interest for late payment. The interest need not be exorbitant—1.5 to 3 percent per month tends to be standard—but it may be enough to jolt a client into realizing that you have not been paid for your work. If nothing else, interest gets the attention of the accounts payable staff at your client's business, goading them into bringing the overdue invoice to your client's attention. In such cases, the client may call to negotiate the interest away in exchange for prompt (albeit already late) payment.

Accept Credit Cards

Sometimes, especially if you specialize in start-up businesses, a client may not have the cash on hand to write you a check—but she will be happy to put your fee on a credit card for her to pay off later. This is a win-win situation, in that you get your payment without her having to relinquish cash she may need for her payroll.

Until very recently, the high monthly fees and transaction minimums credit card companies required made it cost-prohibitive for one-person businesses to accept credit cards. With the boom in at-home businesses and small companies, however, it's now possible for any business to accept credit cards and process the transactions by phone. Monthly fees can be as low as $5 (some services have no monthly fees at all), and there may be a nominal, one-time setup fee to get you started. There's still a small percentage charge for each transaction, but the opportunity to receive immediate payment from a client may make this fee seem nominal.

Take a look at Accept-by-Phone.com, Intelli-collect.com, Propay.com, Charge.com, or others to understand the options available to you as a small business. While it's tough to make an apples-to-apples comparison because rate structures vary from one service to another, each of these offers solid options for your one-person company.

Estimating Your Costs

Nearly every project you take on requires an estimate, a well-informed price quote that lets your client know what it will cost to work with you. Estimating the time required for a job can be very tricky, however, if you've never had to calculate the amount of time you will need to do a thorough, complete job on a project. In addition, many jobs also involve subcontractors and other out-of-pocket expenses for which you will need outside estimates from your trusted suppliers.

It's important to understand that your clients will hold you to your estimate, no matter how off-the-wall the bottom line may be. If your estimate says that you will handle nationwide media relations for your client's mass-market consumer product for the appallingly low sum of $300 per month, your client will expect you to do so—even if you discover later that you're really spending $2,000 of your time per month to do the job. There's no easy way to raise your price at that point unless your client has drastically changed the parameters of the project. You gave him a dirt-low estimate, and now you're stuck with doing the job at a desperately inadequate rate of pay.

Good estimating skills become a critical part of making your business successful. The process will become second nature to you in a fairly short time, but it's good to have a list of the kinds of questions you need to ask your client to prepare a solid, dependable estimate. This list will help get you started.

Questions for Estimates

1. **What is the project's objective?** This helps you determine what the client hopes to accomplish, and how you and the client will tell if the project has been a success.
2. **What tactics do you expect to use throughout the course of the project?** The client may expect you to come back to him with a proposal that lists the tactics you recommend, but it's good to know what activities he expects you to include.
3. **What is the scope of the project**—is it local, regional, national or international?
4. **Will the project reach a mass-market audience, or a niche audience?** If it's a niche, how big is the potential audience?
5. **Who are the decision-makers on the client's team?** The more people who are involved in the approval stream, the longer and more complex the project is likely to be.
6. **What is the ultimate time frame for the project?** It may be short term, longer term, or ongoing with no definite end date.
7. **What are the deliverables?** You may create a press kit, a brochure, a media list, a mailing package, a website, a Facebook fan page, or other promotional tools.
8. **What quantities of each piece are required?** If you need to get print estimates, this is the first question the printer will ask you.
9. **Is there travel involved in the project?** If so, most agencies bill travel time at half their normal billable rate, and travel expenses at cost with no markup.
10. **What is the client's available budget for this project?** Knowing up front what the client expects to spend will help you determine the services you can offer within his available funds. If the client's budget is extraordinarily low for the scope and time frame, now is the time to tell him so, and to begin to set appropriate expectations for what you can accomplish.

What should an estimate look like? This document represents you as a professional, and it may be the only exposure you will receive with decision-makers throughout a client's company. Delivering a polished, authoritative-looking estimate will help you make a positive impression on people whom you may not meet until you win the job.

Here is a sample format and language with which I have had excellent success. Use your electronic letterhead to feature your logo at the top. Make sure you have space for signatures at the bottom of the estimate—it's unwise to start any project without your client's written authorization to do so.

Sample Estimate Form

[Your logo, address, phone and e-mail]   [Date]

Prepared for:
[Client's name]
[Client's company]

Thank you for the opportunity to provide an estimate for **[client's company] [name of project]**. Based on the needs assessment provided, we believe that **[your company name]** is the right fit as your cost-effective, comprehensive solution for your public relations requirements.

Should you have questions or need clarification on any points in this proposal, I will be happy to provide further documentation, work samples, and any other materials that will be helpful.

I look forward to working with **[client's company]** on a regular basis, and to learning more about **[client's industry]**. Thank you again for considering **[your company name]** for this project.

Sincerely,

[Your name]
[Your title]

This budget is based on the following hourly rates:

[Your name]: $XXX/hour
[Name of graphic artist]: $XX/hour

Press releases. Copywriting and up to three rounds of edits per release. $XXX

Newsletter. Collect all stories and photos from staff, and edit of staff copy to maintain a consistent tone and style throughout the document. Copywriting of up to six stories as needed per issue. Prepare all text and photo files for the graphic artist. X,XXX

Layout of twenty-page newsletter using existing design template. Includes two rounds of changes, any adjustments required to photos for color correction, contrast or alterations, and preparing the files for the printer. X,XXX

Travel tour brochure. Copywriting and editing of a four-panel brochure, including two rounds of edits. XXX

Layout of four-panel brochure. Includes two rounds of changes, any adjustments required to photos for color correction, contrast or alterations, and preparing the files for the printer. XXX

Social media. One month of updates to a Facebook page (five days a week) and a Twitter account, as well as up to four blog entries per month. Includes interviews with staff for content ideas, a planning grid with all topics listed, writing, and one round of edits. Total: Twenty Facebook/Twitter updates and four three-paragraph blogs. XXX

Media relations. Distribution of a news release to area media, and follow-up as appropriate to encourage placement. XXX

Special event media. Development of story ideas for various media outlets, and pitching by e-mail and phone to feature writers and producers. *(Cost may be higher if I need to be on-site to manage the media for a specific placement.)* XXX

Please note: **A monthly installment (retainer) amount will depend on the number of each of these projects required in a six-month period. For the sake of discussion, we have based our quote on the following breakdown for six months. If this list overestimates or underestimates the work required, we will be happy to provide a more accurate estimate.**

10 news releases	X,XXX
2 issues of newsletter	X,XXX
2 events or educational programs	X,XXX
1 travel tour brochure	XXX
6 months of social media	X,XXX
2 media relations for special events	XXX
10 news releases sent with follow-up	XXX
I media list transfer/update	XXX
6-month total	$XX,XXX
Cost per month for 6 months	**$X,XXX**

Terms:

- [Your company name] will invoice the client on the first of each month for work completed in the preceding month.

- Payment is due net thirty days from date of invoice.

- A 3 percent interest charge per month will be added to invoices that are not paid within thirty days.

Approval to proceed:

_____   _____
[Your name and company]   Date

_____   _____
[Client's name and company]   Date

When the Project Changes

Some projects begin as one thing, and morph slowly into another, larger thing as time goes on. When this happens, you may find yourself doing far more work than you had anticipated, and certainly more than your budget estimate predicted.

The most ethical clients will know that the scope change means an increase in your fees, and will ask you for an estimate to cover the new elements within the project. Clients who are less scrupulous, however, may never bring it up—and they will feign astonishment when you send them an invoice for an amount several times higher than your original estimate.

Remember that you are the only person who represents your best interests, so when the project changes, it's up to you to tell your client it's time to re-estimate the hours and effort required. Your statement can be simple: "We originally planned on three releases, but now we're talking about seven. I'll give you a new estimate to reflect this change, so you'll have it for your budgeting purposes." Don't ask permission to submit an estimate; tell your client that you will do it, as if it's standard procedure for your company (and it is!). Then do it as quickly as possible—the same day or the following day. This will keep everyone's financial house in order while ensuring that you will be paid fairly for the work required. Finally, make sure your client signs the revised estimate, so you have proof that he authorized the additional expenditure.

Cattle Calls: The Request for Proposal

If you do a lot of government or corporate work, chances are good that you will receive the occasional weighty document titled Request for Proposal (RFP) or Request for Quote (RFQ). Government agencies in particular are required to receive multiple bids on every job for which they hire outside contractors. Large corporations, non-profit organizations, and even some smaller manufacturing or service businesses will issue RFPs or RFQs for all kinds of jobs, from construction to communications.

When you receive an RFP, your immediate reaction may be excitement that you have been included in a round-robin agency search. As you look at the requirements more closely, however, you may find that your response to the RFP requires a great deal of time and effort to complete. Before you plunge headlong into the process, let's discuss some of the pros and cons of the RFP cycle.

The good news: Your one-person company came to the surface when the department in question prepared a list of agencies to solicit for responses. You're on their

Debug

SWAG Estimates

Sometimes a client has no idea what a project will entail, and will look to you to determine the tactics involved. Other clients may come to you to run the media relations for a major event, coordinate a shareholders' meeting, or handle the launch of a new store location. In such instances, it can be nearly impossible to determine how many hours will be required to bring the project to successful completion.

You may find yourself putting together what contractors of all stripes call a SWAG estimate—an acronym for "Some Wild-Ass Guess." When you know that the scope will change over time and you can't predict what may be involved—even after asking tons of questions—you can get your arms around the real project parameters by breaking down the work into two phases: planning and execution.

- **Planning:** Ask the client to pay you a comparatively nominal fee for ten to fifteen hours of your time, so that you can write a communications plan for the event or project. The planning process will involve a couple of meetings with the client's staff and a review of their existing public relations materials and plans, after which you will write a comprehensive plan for your work on the project.

- **Execution:** When the client and other decision-makers have reviewed the plan and chosen the tactics they want you to handle for them, complete an itemized estimate for these elements. You will have a much greater command of the budget when you know exactly what you're being asked to do.

If you don't have the luxury of asking for a planning budget because of the proposal's parameters, end the estimate with a statement that these figures are provided for discussion purposes only: "At the end of this discovery phase, [Your Company Name] will provide an updated estimate based on the fully defined job requirements."

radar, which means that even if you don't win in this round, you may be asked to participate again if your proposal impresses the decision-makers. Chances are there's a significant budget involved—most organizations will not go through the RFP process unless there's a good chunk of money at stake.

The not-as-good news: You may be one of dozens of agencies to receive this RFP, because the people making the list used the Yellow Pages or a Google search of all the agencies in a specific geographic area. This is why we refer to many RFPs as "cattle calls." That being said, not all of them will respond—in fact, the vast majority will not. Current workloads, a lack of a logical match with an agency's core strengths, or a general dislike of working with government or nonprofit organizations all may discourage an agency from assigning its people to a lengthy RFP response process.

The bad news: Many RFPs are already "wired" from the inside. The client already knows which agency will be hired to do the work, but the organization must go through the motions to fulfill its legal obligation to get three or more competitive bids. Worse, the client will not tell you that this is the case, because wiring the bid is essentially illegal for government jobs. (A corporation or nonprofit organization, however, may have no such ethical considerations.)

So how do you protect yourself from spending countless hours on an RFP response when the deck may be stacked against you? Before you start, ask all the questions you can. Keep in mind that the client may share your questions and answers with everyone involved in the RFP process, including the other responders—i.e., your competitors. This is standard procedure, especially for government organizations, as they believe that this keeps one agency from gaining a competitive advantage over the others. Sadly, a competitive advantage is exactly what you had in mind.

Based on the answers you receive, you may feel encouraged to put in the time required to respond. Small agencies do win these bids—in fact, sometimes a sole proprietor is exactly what these organizations want, because of the one-on-one working relationship they can enjoy. You and your company may be preferable to the "pitch and ditch" phenomenon that happens when a large agency sends in the CEO for the pitch meetings, then hands the project off to a low-level account executive who does not have the depth of experience the client thought he was buying.

It's also possible that you will submit your beautiful, well-considered RFP response and never hear from the organization again. All too often, no follow-up takes place with the agencies that are rejected in the first round, so you don't even receive a letter acknowledging your efforts. In other cases, the project gets postponed

In addition to specific questions about the project scope that are not clear in the RFP document, ask these questions to get a sense of the competitive field.

1. How many agencies have been asked to respond to the RFP?
2. How many have indicated that they will actually provide a response?
3. Can you share with me who the other responding agencies are? (They may say no to this, but it can't hurt to ask.)
4. How was my company chosen to receive this RFP?
5. Is location a factor in choosing the agency for your project? (This is particularly important if the client is in a different city or state.)
6. Is agency size a factor?
7. If so, how likely is it that a one-person firm will be selected?
8. What is the time frame for making your selection, once you have received all the responses?
9. How soon after that will the work begin?
10. Do you have a specific budget figure in mind for the project?
11. Do you already have a specific agency in mind for this project? I know that you are required to get competitive bids, but is there an agency with whom you work regularly?
12. If you have a long-term working relationship with an agency and you are not required by law to get bids, why are you looking for a new firm with this RFP? (This may uncover the "pain points" the client may have with the agency in place.)

or canceled because of budget constraints or a need to shift focus to something more pressing . . . and the organization does not bother to notify the RFP participants. This is inconsiderate and classless, to say the least, but it's standard procedure in many instances. If you don't hear anything beyond whatever schedule the RFP outlined, you have the right to call and find out what happened to your proposal and to the project.

When Clients Don't Pay

By and large, the vast majority of clients expect to pay you for the work you do for them. Most will pay on time. Some even pay early, because they understand that you work for yourself and maintaining good cash flow allows you to pay your own bills promptly. Others may require a little extra time, or they may have restrictive payment terms that they impose on their vendors, informing them that they pay all invoices in forty-five to sixty days instead of the standard thirty days.

A handful of others, however, simply won't pay their bills. Some are otherwise honest people who run into hard times during a down economy. Others are contrarians who tell you that they don't feel that they should have to pay as much as you charge, well after they signed your estimate. Some may question how much work you actually did, claiming they really did it all themselves because they had to spend so much time working with you on the project (all those interviews and meetings while you gathered information).

A select few simply steal your services and disappear. The short list of the most notorious includes start-up businesses working from a mobile phone and a coffee shop, local political candidates (especially those who lose), and transient event managers. Even large, well-established companies can fall into the non-payment category when top management makes a series of catastrophic mistakes that plunge the company into insurmountable debt.

As a one-person business, your options for collecting on long overdue debts can be very limited. Here's a process to help you determine just how bad this bad debt has become.

Call the Client
It's always possible that an invoice has been mislaid, or that a client is waiting for a big check to come in and can't pay you until it arrives. If the latter is the case, it's too bad he didn't tell you that up front, but he still has every intention of paying you when the money comes in. (I once waited five months for a $40,000 check from a client, but he kept in touch with me on a weekly basis until his venture capital came in and he could pay me. I got every cent.)

Send a Past Due Invoice
Go to your favorite office supplies store and buy a big red stamp that says "Past Due" in large warning letters. Add an interest charge to the invoice to be sure the client sees the penalty for non-payment.

Call Again
If there's an accounts payable department at your client's place of business, call them and ask why your invoice has not been paid. (Note that the people who run this desk

often are experts at dodging calls like yours.) If your client has really run into financial difficulties, the company owes it to you to explain. Once you get a human being on the phone, offer to set up a payment plan. Confirm the plan in writing once you've come to an agreement.

Still No Luck?

If it's a large enough invoice to warrant it, have your attorney send a letter to your client, detailing the legal steps you are willing to take to get paid. Getting a letter from an attorney may be just the kick in the pants your client needs to take action on the late payment.

Take Him to Court

Depending on the size of the amount in arrears, you can file a claim with the small claims court in your city or county. Top limits vary by state, but if your claim is a few thousand dollars or less, small claims court can be a cost-effective option. You can make your case if you can prove that the client expected to pay—this is why you need your estimates signed by the client—and that you completed the work to the client's satisfaction. Save every e-mail you receive acknowledging receipt of your work, discussing edits and next steps, and praising your excellent skills. All of these will help you make the case that the payment you've invoiced is due to you. If the court rules in your favor, the court will serve your client with the judgment against him, and he will have a set time (usually twenty-one to thirty days) in which to pay you. You will be responsible for collecting on the debt, but you will have the law on your side.

There's one drawback to small claims court: You need to file your claim in the court that has jurisdiction over the municipality in which your client's company resides. If you do a lot of business out of state, this requires that you travel for your court date. If you don't show up for the court date, you lose the case.

Hire a Collection Agency

If you don't want to involve the court, you can try to find a collection agency that will take on a single account for a small business. You will pay a significant percentage of the invoice—up to a third—for the privilege of having this agency harass your client on your behalf. Even if a collection agency advertises that it serves small businesses, however, the staff's attention will focus on larger accounts with big potential payouts, so your little invoice may fall to the bottom of the pile. You will need to check with the agency on a regular basis to be sure there's someone there who is actively pursuing your client.

Some Debts are Uncollectable

Your client may be in such dire financial straits that he truly cannot afford to pay you. If there is no blood to wring from this stone, you may be forced to forget about collecting on this invoice.

In this case, one of several things may happen. First, the client may sell the company to get out from under this and all of his other debts. At the end of the lengthy sale process, the new owner will be responsible for paying off the debts of the business it has just acquired. You should be contacted by the new owners, but if you do not hear from them, follow up to be sure they have your invoice among the debts to be paid off. Months may go by before you receive the payment, but chances are good that you will eventually see the check in the mail.

Alternately, a client's bankruptcy filing may be close at hand. If the client declares bankruptcy or goes into receivership and names you as one of its many creditors, his obligation to pay you is eliminated by the court proceeding. Essentially, the law dictates that he no longer owes you the money, so it's time to let go of the anger and betrayal you feel about not receiving your payment, and move on to more lucrative clients. Believe me, this client has suffered plenty as he watched his business fail and dissolve away; he even may have lost his personal property in the process.

I want to close this section with a positive story about my husband's business, Nic Minetor Lighting. Several years ago, Nic provided the lighting for an event run by a local production company, but when his invoice hadn't been paid after ninety days, I took up the role of collection hound on his behalf. The production company's owner was extremely apologetic, but when his client had paid him for his work, he had used the money to pay his own mortgage and other personal bills. A year later he landed in bankruptcy court, and we wrote off his debt. We assumed that was the end of the saga.

Three years later, with no preamble, Nic received a check in the mail from the same production company owner, for the full amount of Nic's invoice! I ran into this man in a local Starbucks a week later, and thanked him for the payment. "You know you didn't have to do that," I said.

He replied, "Oh yes, for my own peace of mind, I did have to do that."

The moral of the story: Good people get into financial trouble occasionally, and some of them do things that restore your faith in the rest.

07

Money: How to Manage It

Whether you are a sole proprietor or you've incorporated your business, you need to manage your income and expenses according to the basic tenets of bookkeeping and accounting. You don't need to take a course in corporate financial management, but you do need to know where your money is, how much you need to pay your bills, and how much your clients owe you at any given moment.

Start by opening a business bank account in your firm's name. Tax law requires corporations to maintain a business checking account, but even a sole proprietorship needs its own account, so you can separate your business expenses cleanly from your personal expenses. This will make it very easy to claim the business expenses on Schedule C of your income tax return.

If you're a sole proprietor and you would rather stick with your personal checking account instead of maintaining two accounts, keep careful records of your income and expenditures related to your business. It's much tougher to prove that you had business expenses if the transactions are intermingled with your personal and household purchases.

Daily Money Management

First, choose a money management software package designed for small businesses. QuickBooks, Peachtree, Bookkeeper, AccountEdge, iBank, Gnu-Cash, and NetSuite are a few of the names you will see as you consider your options. Check with your accountant to see which packages are compatible with the software the firm uses. When you both use the same software, you can exchange files smoothly during tax return preparation time.

A good money management program gives you the ability to do many things that you and your accountant need:

- Track your checking account debits and credits, and balance your account in minutes.
- Generate reports including profit and loss, trial balance, general ledger, sales, receivables, payables, and transaction records.
- Track your sales tax liability, and provide an instant report of the amount you owe.
- Provide time tracking, allowing you to record the time spent on each job per day, and how that time was used.
- Link your hours with client jobs, and transfer that time into the correct invoices.
- Track your reimbursable expenses, link them to the right jobs, and transfer these expenses into the correct invoices.
- Download transactions from your bank and credit card companies directly into the right registers.
- Create invoices and print envelopes or mailing labels for prompt mailing.
- Generate a report of pending client invoices, with the amount each owes you and the due date.
- Track your bills and alert you when bills are due.
- Calculate payroll, even if you are the only employee.

Debug

Secure Your Account Numbers

You may be tempted to record all of your checking, savings, and credit card account numbers within your money management software or elsewhere on your computer. Don't do it! If you work from a laptop and a thief steals it, he will have access to your account numbers, and you could become a victim of identity theft. Even if the thief simply pawns your computer without raiding your records, you will need to cancel all of your credit cards and other accounts as a precaution. Save yourself the trouble and keep your account numbers off your computer.

Setting Up Your Company

When you've installed your new software, start by establishing all of your business **accounts:** checking, savings, credit cards, line of credit, and any others through which your money will flow.

Next, make a list of **items:** the services you provide to your clients. As a public relations business owner, your items may include some or all of the ones listed here. You also may have specialized services related to your areas of expertise.

- Account management
- Client meeting
- Copywriting
- Editing
- Interviews
- Media list building
- Media relations
- Online monitoring
- Proofreading
- PR consulting
- Production
- Research
- Trade show attendance
- Travel time

You will be prompted to determine what you will charge for each service. For most activities, stick to the hourly rate you've already chosen for all of your client work. Some things, however, may warrant that you charge a higher or lower rate. Public relations consulting, for example, often takes place at higher levels of a client company, so you may have the opportunity to charge more for this service. Proofreading, on the other hand, may be a task for which you need to charge less to be competitive with people who proofread full-time (generally for a much lower hourly rate than you charge for your services). When traveling to a trade show or a remote client site, most agencies bill their travel time at half the hourly rate.

Next, set up your list of **customers.** If you don't have any clients yet, you can do this as you bring in business. Larger agencies assign each client a number, and then use this number as a prefix as they add jobs (so, for example, Associated Paint Company becomes client number 100; a product launch news release for Associated Paint is number 100-001). You don't need to do this for your one-person business unless you're so used to this kind of system that you won't be comfortable without it.

For each client, fill in the screen with the name, company name, address, and so on, so all of this information will appear on each invoice. As you begin a new assignment, create a new job under the client's name in the customer list. Each software package does this differently, so if the "Add Job" button does not show itself immediately, search the help section to find out where it is.

Now, create an **account** for each of your regular vendors. At the outset, these may include your mobile phone and Internet service providers, your business insurance company, your health insurance company (if the business pays for this), your accountant and attorney, a media research and news release distribution company (PRWeb, PR Newswire, or whichever you choose), and other vendors you pay on a monthly basis. If you fill in the address and account number blanks, your software will print this information on the checks you create to pay your bills. Alternately, you can pay almost all of your bills online, and virtually eliminate the need for checks.

When you complete all of these lists, you're ready to start entering your income and expense information.

Do It Every Day

What is the biggest complaint home-based businesspeople have about running their businesses? Most lament the pile of receipts, bills, and statements in their IN boxes, explaining that they hate the data entry and find the growing pile "just too overwhelming" to tackle. As a result, they make late payments on their bills, struggle to get invoices out to clients in a timely manner, and never know quite how much money they have on hand at any given time. Worse, expenses that should be reimbursed by a client get lost in the pile, becoming uncollectable after a project's final invoice has already gone out.

You can avoid all of these issues by developing one simple habit: Make financial management a five-minutes-a-day task.

Every day, put five minutes aside to open the mail, find the bills, and enter the amounts and due dates into your money management program. Take all of the receipts out of your wallet or purse and enter any that relate to your business into your checking or credit card registers. Of course, record your hours throughout the day as we discussed in chapter 6, noting the job, your activity, and how much time you spent on that task.

File your receipts and bills immediately—it will only take a second—or make PDFs of them by scanning them onto your hard drive.

If you do your financial data entry every day, you'll deal with no more than three or four transactions a day on average, and you'll eliminate the menacing buildup on that scary corner of your desk. Make it a habit from your first day in business.

Projecting Income and Cash Flow

Do you need more business, or will your current workload cover your expenses and help you reach your financial goals? You may feel like you've got all you can handle, but the work on your desk today may or may not generate the income you require.

Generally, your public relations business does not require a lot of up-front expenses in your work for clients. You have few supplies to buy on your clients' behalf, and while you may have to front the cost of news release distribution using an online service, this expense tends to come at the end of a project, so you can bill it to the client in short order. Rarely will you be faced with a "cash poor" situation in which you've spent thousands of dollars on materials that depleted your cash on hand.

Your largest expenses, then, are your own salary and your income taxes (more on these in chapter 8). There's nothing worse than reaching the end of the month and discovering that you cannot make the next month's mortgage payment because you didn't foresee a gap in your cash flow. If you depend on your business for your household's income, you must do your best to know well in advance if you need to hustle to bring in more business, or if your current efforts will cover your expense requirements.

In addition, some months require more money than others. Paying your business insurance premiums, your accountant's fee for doing your corporate taxes, and your subscription fee for your media research service can all come at the same time, especially if you initiated all of these things in your first month in business. Knowing when this money crunch will hit gives you the ability to plan ahead, take on additional business in anticipation of the load, and cover all of these expenses while still paying yourself regularly.

The following worksheet will help make your cash flow projections quick and easy. Set this up as a spreadsheet on your computer, or use this as a template to populate the cash flow forecasting tool in your financial management software program.

Cash Flow Projection

	January	February	March	Q1 Totals
Cash on hand				
Receivables				
Total available cash				
Expenses				
Gross salary, including income taxes				
Office supplies				
Professional services (accountant, attorney, etc.)				
Repairs and maintenance				
Promotion and advertising (including website fees)				
Vehicle (payments, maintenance, and gas)				
Travel and entertainment				
Phone and Internet				
Insurance				
Printing and reproduction				
Postage and shipping				
Dues and subscriptions				
Debt service (credit card payments)				
Reference materials				
Services purchased from vendors (graphic design, web development, etc.)				
TOTAL CASH PAID				
Income/Deficit *(Subtract Total Cash Paid from Total Available Cash)*				

Your Starting Capital

Even a low-overhead business like a home-based public relations firm requires some money to get started, and the sources for this money tend to fall into some pretty narrow categories.

A study completed by the Kaufmann Foundation revealed that in 2004, 75 percent of start-up businesses use the owner's money as their initial capital. Only about 5 percent look to spouses and parents for loans, but as many as 25 percent rely on personal credit cards for their start-up financing. Very few new businesses take on financial investors to get their working capital. Instead, five times as many new businesses borrow money from the outside—i.e., from banks—and have this debt to pay back as their business grows.

Saddling your business with outside debt right from the start can severely limit your ability to take chances, put non-billable time into marketing and developing a specialty, or take advantage of the flexibility your home-based business can provide. I urge you to finance your new business from your personal savings rather than with credit cards, bank loans, or even loans from family members. Remember the calculations you made back in chapter 4 when you wrote your business plan—you know how much money you need to make the best possible start, so determine how much of this can come from your own funds, and how much may have to come from other sources.

When you borrow from your own funds, the business can pay you back for this investment tax-free once you've started to make some real money. The debt to yourself appears as a "loan from officer" in your list of accounts, and paying back that loan can happen on any schedule that makes sense for you and your business.

If you just don't have the cash on hand, the US Small Business Administration (SBA) can help you find a lender through its Guaranteed Loan Programs. The SBA does not make direct loans to small businesses, but it can guide you in finding its lending partners that provide commercial loans structured according to the SBA's specific requirements. The SBA then guarantees payment on these loans. To connect with the SBA, visit www.sba.gov and click on "Our Offices" to find the location nearest you. Your bank may have a loan officer on staff who handles SBA loans, so if you've established a business checking account and a relationship with a local bank branch, this might be a good place to start investigating the possibility of a loan as well. Such loans come with low interest rates and a fixed monthly payment, allowing you to plan your monthly expenses predictably.

Credit card financing should be a last resort, but if you must go this way, do it in increments: Buy just what you need in a given month, and pay off the credit card completely when the bill comes. If you can ramp up your business this way over the course of several months, you won't accumulate a big, high-interest debt that becomes the central motivating factor for bringing in work.

Establishing Business Credit

One day, when your business is well established and everyone in your specialty knows your name, you will enjoy a substantial cash reserve from which you can draw when you need to take on expenses at the beginning of a client's project, upgrade your office equipment, or pay vendors when a client's check does not arrive on time.

In the interim, however, you will need to establish credit for your business. It takes time to do this, as few banks or credit card companies get excited about offering credit to start-up businesses. The fact is that many start-ups default on their loans and credit cards, which spoils the field for the rest of us who plan to prosper and make our payments on time.

When you apply for business credit, credit card companies and banks begin to consider your application by validating your business information. You can take steps to make your business picture look as appealing as possible.

- Establishing a corporation or limited liability company (LLC) turns your business into its own entity, separate from you and your personal credit history—an important first step in acquiring business credit. It may be harder to get a business credit card if your business is a sole proprietorship.
- Get a federal Employer Identification Number (EIN), which you will need anyway to file taxes.
- Open a business bank account in your company's legal name.
- Get a dedicated telephone line for your business. If this is your mobile phone, answer the phone with your business name ("Minetor and Company, this is Randi") during business hours.

Now your potential creditors can see that your business actually exists. If you've paid your bills on time since you founded the business, you are closer to receiving the credit you need.

Business Credit Card or Line of Credit

Banks can offer you the option of either a credit card or a business line of credit. There are some significant differences between the two.

A **credit card** gives you a set credit limit and all the convenience of using it in stores, when you travel, and online. Once you have the card, you can charge whatever you choose, pay down the balance, and use it again. The trade-off for all this convenience, of course, is an interest rate that may skyrocket suddenly with little warning if you make a payment a day late, a major problem if you're carrying a large balance.

Some lenders offer low-interest introductory deals on credit cards, and bonuses like cash back on your purchases or affinity points that you can use toward travel and purchases. American Express, Capital One, and Chase Bank, for example, are all famous for their offers to small businesses, so these may be good companies to check for competitive rates.

A business **line of credit** is an account with a pre-set credit limit, like a credit card, but usually with a much lower interest rate that remains stable through the life of the account (as long as you make your payments on time). You do not receive a card, so you can't use your line of credit with the freedom with which you use a credit card. In most cases, you receive a small number of checks when you open your line of credit, with the understanding that you will use these for major one-time purchases or the expenses of business growth. (You can reorder checks at any time, of course.) Your business line of credit offers an option that emphasizes control and sparing use, with the assumption that you will use the money only when you have receivables with which you can pay off the balance in short order.

In the post-2008 environment, banks have reined in their approval of lines of credit for small businesses. There seems to be no shortage of credit card offers, however, so even if you prefer the more conservative option of the line of credit, you may have better luck obtaining a credit card in the current economic climate.

08 | Taxes and Records

Few things frighten new at-home business owners as deeply as the concept of dealing with the federal tax code. Add to this the layers of city, borough, county, or state taxes that may be required in your place of residence, and you have a nightmarish jumble that provides any number of opportunities to make expensive mistakes. The tax code is every bit as complex as politicians, bureaucrats, and accountants say it is—and there's no good reason to spend your time learning chapter and verse of this dismal doctrine. That's why you have an accountant among your trusted advisors.

If you're a sole proprietor, LLC, or an S corporation and you will fill out a Schedule C when you file your Form 1040 income tax return, however, you do need a working familiarity with your tax obligations and how your taxes will be paid. It also helps to know what expenses can be deducted from your income as legitimate business expenses, so you will save the right statements and receipts to hand over to your accountant at tax time.

Estimated Quarterly Taxes

As an independent business owner, you are required to pay income taxes, Social Security, and Medicare taxes, just as you did while you worked for someone else. The difference, of course, is that no one is taking them out for you before you get your money, so you need to know exactly how much of your money you can keep, and how much you need to set aside to pay to the government at the end of the quarter.

To determine how much tax you need to pay, use the IRS Form 1040-ES, Estimated Tax. (You can download this form as a PDF at www.irs.gov/pub/irs-pdf/f1040es.pdf.) Your tax rate is determined by your net profit from your business, so you will need to calculate this. The process seems fairly easy at first: Subtract your expenses from your income. Needless to say, that's not how it appears on Form 1040-ES; instead, this calculation becomes staggeringly complex. Go through the worksheet carefully to reach an adjusted gross income figure, which goes on line 1 of the second worksheet. Then add up your itemized deductions—your business expenses—and enter them on line 2. Now you have your net profit or loss, but the calculations continue through a total of seventeen lines to establish what you actually owe in taxes. If you're determined not to use an accountant to figure these taxes for you, I highly recommend at least a tutorial session with your accountant, to be sure that you're making these calculations correctly. Penalties can be stiff on payments that are too low.

Pay your taxes by sending in the 1040-ES form with a check, or make your payments online at the Electronic Federal Tax Payment System (EFTPS) at www.eftps .gov/eftps/.

The Self-Employment Tax

When I first went into business, I sent an e-mail to all of my friends to let them know that I'd launched Minetor & Company. The vast majority sent back messages of congratulations and encouragement, but one lone self-employed writer on the West Coast responded entirely differently. "Wait until you see how much you have to pay in self-employment taxes," he said.

I took a bit of offense at the time, but several months later I understood his warning.

As business owners, we are required to pay the taxes our employers paid on our behalf. This may come as a shock if you didn't know that your employer paid additional taxes beyond those taken out of your paycheck. Essentially, employees pay half of the required Social Security (SSI) and Medicare taxes, while employers pay the other half. This means that you, as a self-employed person, pay both the employer and employee share of the Social Security and Medicare taxes—double the SSI and Medicare. You pay this additional tax if your income from your business exceeds $400 in a calendar year.

Make these payments as part of your quarterly estimated tax payments. If you run a very profitable business, you pay more over time, just as you pay more in federal and state income tax. If your business takes a while to get off the ground, your self-employment tax payments may be negligible.

There is a bit of good news in all this: According to current tax law as I write this, once your income reaches $106,800 in a single year, you no longer need to pay Social Security tax for that year. I'm sure you will agree that this is a noble goal.

If your company is a C corporation, you will pay your income taxes on a monthly basis, on or before the 15th of the following month. You will also file quarterly employer tax returns, using Form 941, Employer's Quarterly Federal Tax Return. As most self-employed PR professionals do not incorporate as C corporations, I refer you to the comprehensive IRS site for more information on this: www.irs.gov/businesses/small/article/0,,id=98240,00.html.

Filing Your Annual Income Taxes

To file your annual income tax return, you will need to itemize all of the business expenses you added up for your estimated quarterly taxes. The list of expenses—totaled by category—goes on Schedule C of your annual return. The grand total of these expenses gets subtracted from the total of your gross income. Whatever remains is your net profit, on which you pay your annual income taxes.

If you've been diligent in calculating your estimated taxes each quarter, you will have no additional taxes to pay; you may even receive a refund.

In addition to the Schedule C, you need to file a 1040 Schedule SE (Self-Employment), which determines if you have paid enough SSI and Medicare in the previous year. You may have to make an additional payment here if your income exceeded your estimates on your quarterly returns. It's also possible that you will receive a refund for overpayment.

Filing Your Corporate Tax Return

If you have incorporated your business, you will need to file a separate tax return for your business at the end of your fiscal year. Use US Income Tax Return for an S Corporation Form 1120S if your firm is an S corporation, with the addition of a Schedule K-1 Form to report your share of the company's income. C corporations use US Corporate Income Tax Return Form 1120.

The complexities of these forms and the US corporate tax code will monopolize a great deal of your time—time you could be spending generating new business or completing work for clients. While an accountant's fees for preparing corporate tax returns can rise into the four-figure level, it's money well spent to keep you and your business compliant with the law and out of the IRS searchlight.

What about Those Computer Software Packages That Do Your Taxes?

You may feel that you will save a great deal of money if you do your own taxes using one of the programs designed for this purpose. While people with some experience with the vocabulary and concepts involved in accounting have some luck with these, those of us with little background in bookkeeping and no clear understanding of the tax code find these more confusing than useful. (You are welcome to disregard my opinion, of course, and try one for yourself.) As tax law changes every year, these packages are only useful for one tax season; next year, you'll have to purchase the new version. The potential for costly mistakes can be very high when you apply your general inexperience to the task, so if you attempt this and you don't like the results, be prepared to make the additional investment in your accountant's time. An accountant who specializes in small businesses will know exactly how to do the most thorough, accurate job for you.

Business Use of Your Home

Many people tell me that they decided to work from home because of the great tax deductions they could take by using their home for business. While tax deductions are indeed available for this, it's critical that you use the business-related parts of your home in the correct ways to be sure that you qualify for these deductions. Here are the IRS's stringent requirements.

Exclusive Use

The area that you deduct must be used exclusively for business. If you've converted a guest room into an office, this room must remain an office all the time—you can't reconvert it into a bedroom when your son comes home from college. The same goes for multiple-use spaces: If you're using a portion of the garage as your office, set up partitions to create a clear delineation between the part that provides shelter for your vehicles and the part that serves as your office.

Your deduction is for the exact square footage of the space you have made a permanent office. If the total footprint of your house is 2,000 square feet, and you are using 100 square feet as your office space, your office space comprises 5 percent of your total home. You can deduct 5 percent of the cost of your mortgage, mortgage interest, and real estate taxes as a Schedule C business expense. If you've paid off your mortgage, you can still deduct this percentage of your real estate taxes.

Regular Use

If your workspace is part of a room that's used for other things, you can still take the deduction if you use that space on a regular basis, i.e., daily, weekly, or monthly, for about the same amount of time in each interval.

Principal Place of Business

If you are working from home full-time, your home qualifies as your principal place of business. If you are working on a contract basis for one client who provides you with an office at his place of business, your home office may not qualify for the deduction.

Separate Structures

Perhaps you've created your home office in another structure on your property: a guesthouse, a detached garage, a large shed, or a barn. You can take the deduction for the use of this space as part of your overall residential property.

Other Defendable Expenses

In addition to your mortgage and real estate tax deduction, percentages of a number of other expenses can be deducted as well. These include your homeowner's insurance, utilities, home security system, and home repairs or renovation that affect the space in which you do business. Talk to your accountant about the percentages of each of these that are legitimate business deductions in your case.

Business Use of Your Car

The IRS considers any vehicle under six thousand pounds as a car, so whether you drive something as small as a Smart Car or as big as a Ford Expedition, your car should be within the weight limit. You can take a deduction for using your car for business, provided that the use is "ordinary and necessary," according to the tax code. Generally, any driving you do for your business will fall within these two stipulations—you must meet with clients, attend events, make visits for new business opportunities, shop for office supplies, and so on. All of these things are legitimate business transportation expenses.

For your car to qualify for the greatest possible deduction, you must be able to prove that more than 50 percent of its use is for business. Keep a mileage log to track your business versus personal use of the vehicle—a simple pocket-sized notebook will do. When you get into the car to drive to a business meeting or function, record the odometer mileage in the book. When you return home, record the ending mileage. Write down where you went during that interval, and subtract the starting mileage from the ending mileage to get the total mileage for that trip.

In addition, you have the option of deducting expenses like car repairs and gas instead of taking the mileage deduction. Check with your accountant or

Mileage Log

Date	Starting Mileage	Ending Mileage	Total	Destination

the IRS to find out this year's allowable deduction per mile, and calculate which deduction is larger: your total mileage for the year, or the total of your gas, repairs, and maintenance.

Recordkeeping: What to Keep, What to Toss

No matter what expenses qualify for deductions, you will need to prove that you actually spent your money on these things should the IRS ever select you for an audit. Even if you simply receive an inquiry about a specific deduction or a calculation on your return, you will need to have the records on hand to verify the expenses or income you claimed on your return.

The IRS must decide within three years of receiving your return if your case warrants an audit. At that point, however, the auditor can examine your records as far back as seven years ago. For this reason, you must keep seven years of financial records on hand, even though you may never need to look at them again.

What do you need to keep? The IRS will take an interest in any document—statement, receipt, or invoice—that relates to any income or expense that you claimed on your tax returns. For most of us, this whopping pile of paper has no natural resting place in our homes, especially if we must accumulate seven years' worth of the stuff. You have a couple of options for storing all this paper.

1. Set up a shelf unit in your basement, attic, or utility room, and designate it as your long-term file storage area. Make sure it has the capacity to hold seven boxes. When you reach your eighth year, dump out everything in the first box and take it to a commercial shredding company for quick, safe disposal (some of these companies hold a "Community Shredding Day" once or twice a year for small businesses like us, and shred all these documents for free). Use this box for your eighth year's records, and continue this process down the line.

2. If you have nowhere to store these boxes, a sheet-fed scanner is your best friend. The IRS accepts scanned documents as originals, so there's no need to invest real estate in holding on to all these paper files. See chapter 3 for a description of the best way to use a scanner to organize and preserve your documentation.

Running an Ethical PR Business

When my mobile phone rang in the middle of a sunny Sunday afternoon, I knew whatever I heard next would wreak havoc with my weekend plans. Sure enough, the client on the other end spoke so fast that his agitation made me breathless.

"You know that statement I gave you from the dealer in Ohio, saying that he's only specifying our new product and no others?" he said. "Well, he saw it in print and now he's furious. He wants us to retract the quote."

I put the pieces together and suddenly realized what had happened. I had ghostwritten a story for a major trade magazine under my client's byline, and the story included quotes from several dealers about my client's game-changing new product. My client solicited statements from the dealers himself to save a few dollars of the billable time I would have spent interviewing each of them. For the largest dealer in his industry, however, he did not get the statement he gave me from the dealer. Instead, my client made up the quote, figuring that he would ask the dealer's forgiveness rather than permission. I had no idea he'd done that at the time; I had used the quote in the story in good faith.

Now the statement was in print in a monthly magazine read by tens of thousands of people in the industry, and the dealer was outraged. His other suppliers had called him with irate accusations, pointing out—and rightly so—that this dealer specified their products regularly. He had not restricted his business to my client's products at all.

What could I do to help? I suggested to my client that I write a letter to the dealer over his signature, apologizing for the oversight in not checking the quote with him before it went into print.

Before the discussion ended, my client insisted that *I* sign the letter, making the "error" my fault instead of his.

From the Field

Georgi Bohrod, GBG & Associates (www.gbgandassociates.com)

"I can really be who I am."

When the humdinger of all clients came knocking on Georgi Bohrod's door, she just might have taken the job—were it not for a moment of stunning clarity.

This particular client, a lifelong friend in the resort industry, had just bought himself an unusual destination in the state of Nevada: a working brothel. The business was perfectly legal in Nevada, but the astonishing salary he offered and the chance to work at a glamorous retreat frequented by movie stars just couldn't make the idea any more palatable to Bohrod.

"He was moving there to make this his full-time career, and he wanted me to do his PR," Bohrod said, "He invited me up to see the place, and I went. I would have made a fortune! But my first grandchild was on the way, and I said to myself, 'Will I be able to tell this little baby what I do for a living?' So I didn't do it."

She laughs a little wistfully. "If I'd done it, I would have been so loaded! But I couldn't bring myself to do it."

Bohrod's refreshing set of scruples has made her one of the most valued PR practitioners in another trade that raises a few eyebrows: timeshare resorts.

The field became Bohrod's specialty not long after she and her first husband moved to California, when her job at a PR and advertising firm came to an abrupt end. "One day the owners told us, 'We can't stand each other anymore.' They gave us each two weeks' pay and closed up shop," she said. Supporting her husband through law school, and with a young daughter, Bohrod took the first job she was offered: as the PR "gal" at Winners Circle Resorts.

"I threw myself down on the bed and cried that I would have to tell my parents that they spent all this money sending me to Northwestern University, and now I was working for a timeshare," she said.

Despite her misgivings, Bohrod applied herself to the job and soon rose to become the resort's director of marketing. From there, she took her considerable experience in timeshare PR and spun off in her own company, retaining Winners Circle as her first client.

She would do this again with another nationwide timeshare company, working in-house and keeping their business when she returned to her home-based PR firm. By this time, Bohrod had developed a strong reputation as a specialist in timeshare PR, becoming very active in a trade association that gave her a national presence. She happily took on a third of the nation's timeshare PR business, while two other independent practitioners in other areas of the country divide up the rest. "There was always plenty of business to go around between the three of us," she said. "We are the PR people in this industry, we all have different strengths, and people like to work with one or the other of us."

Working from the San Diego home she shares with her present husband, Bohrod has taken over the living room—"we never went in it anyway"—and made it her corporate headquarters. "It's light and airy, and it's the first thing people see when they come over," she said. "It's about 350 square feet, and it works out very well." When clients need to see her, Bohrod travels to their sites, often jetting across the country on short notice. "Our home is just ten minutes from the airport," she said.

While working for resort clients sounds as relaxed as it can get, that's not really the case, she said. "Timeshares have not always had the best reputation," she acknowledged. "I was serving on the Council for Timeshare Excellence, and I had *60 Minutes* coming to a convention. Having them there was pretty nerve-wracking—not because of *60 Minutes,* but in dealing with the personalities who were so afraid of having them there. Another time, one of my clients had been really exposed through social media for not keeping the promises they had made. Some owners threatened to take the information and give it to the media, and they did it. It ended up on the news, on ABC's *20/20.* As PR people, it's our responsibility to take these negative stories and make the outcome as positive as possible. The hardest thing was to educate my clients about that."

In addition to her media skills, Bohrod brings her solid sense of ethics to her timeshare clients. "People need to understand that you're investing in a lifestyle choice," she explained. "We are trying to do a good job of educating the public that you can't sell your timeshare for what you paid for it. You're buying a way of vacationing. People love their timeshares."

Her advice to new home-based PR people? "Have a business plan," she said. "You need a touchstone of where you want to be and what your goals are. It helps you make the big decisions."

I weighed the consequences of not doing as my client asked, determining that while he probably would not fire me outright, my monthly retainer might be severely diminished. Worse than the potential loss of income, however, was the possibility that this dealer—a leading player in my industry of specialization—would take steps to besmirch my reputation for honesty and integrity with my clients. If I did not sign the letter, chances were good that this client would bad-mouth me to the dealer anyway (if he had not already done so), to avoid taking the hit and losing the business. Either way, I was bound to be the loser in this.

I decided that if I were going down, I would go down with the most integrity I could muster. I wrote the letter, signed it, and sent it off to the dealer. A few days later, I received an e-mail from the dealer, thanking me for the letter. "We both know what really happened here, but I appreciate the gesture," he said. The issue remained between us.

My client lost that dealer's business because of a lie he told to get a quote into print, thinking it would help him grow and strengthen his position in the industry. Instead, it had the opposite effect, signaling the beginning of an implosion that would end eleven months later, when he sold his company to a competitor just to get out from under his insurmountable debt.

When a client tells a lie and compounds it with another and another, the aftermath may come to roost at your desk, with the expectation that you can rectify a destructive news cycle and an unending parade of painful headlines. Clients often expect us to have a black bag full of magic out of which we can pull solutions to every kind of challenge, even when they have made dreadful mistakes and bent the public relations code of ethics to the breaking point. There's a bigger question at stake, though: Should you take on the problems that will make you look like a shill for a dishonest individual or corporation?

As a business owner, the decision is yours: You can work with the client to do the right thing and repair the damage to brand and reputation the company may suffer, or you can decline to take on a challenge that has its roots in deceit and denial. Like attorneys, public relations professionals face this dilemma more often than nearly anyone else. When you go into business for yourself, you need to make some critical decisions about the kinds of clients you're willing to represent, and the lengths to which you will go to repair situations in which a client threw his ethics out the window.

Reputation Management Begins at Home

As public relations professionals, gaining the public trust is our stock in trade. Our reputations for honesty and credibility need to be clean as white linen sheets on a country clothesline, or no client will know when they can trust us—and the media will gauge every word we say or write with skepticism. If we're not credible, we cannot represent clients effectively.

What does this mean for you as a business owner? When you approach a relationship with a new client, you want to associate your business with those who reflect your high standards for ethical behavior. Before you enter into an agreement to represent a client, it's up to you to discover all you can about the company and its leadership, to be sure that you have not stumbled into a den of shady business practices.

Everything you need to know is at your fingertips, thanks to the power of online search engines and social networking. Google your potential client's name—both the company name and the CEO or owner—and see what pops up. What issues has this client faced in the past? Look for news stories that discuss lawsuits, legal or customer complaints against the company, personal gaffes in the press, previous bankruptcies, and other issues that raise red flags about honesty and ethical behavior. Check your prospect's blogs, Facebook page, and other social media sites to see what views the company's leadership espouses. If you're working in a specific market niche, search the online editions of trade magazines in that sector to find out what the industry is saying about the company and its products.

In most cases, you'll find that your potential client's company does an honest business with quality products or services, and there have been no legal issues or other problems. Even if you discover a single dust-up, such issues often have perfectly plausible explanations—and you'll know to ask about the incident before you sign a letter of agreement with the client. If the company seems to be pursued by trouble, however, you can rest assured that as the company's public relations contractor, you

Thinkpoint

Above all else, remember that you represent yourself and your own identity first. If you take on a client who does not share your high ethical standards, you could lose your own fine reputation—and forever damage your brand identity.

will become the recipient of all of these tribulations—and you will be expected to "fix" new problems as they arise. Anyone can make a single business mistake, but if you see a pattern, you may want to rethink your approach to this company.

When Clients Want You to Lie

Over the last several decades, the term "PR" has become synonymous with "lie" in the popular vocabulary. We have gone from "flacks" to "spin doctors," people who are believed to hide the truth in flowery language and convoluted messages meant to disguise the facts. When I speak at colleges, at least one student in the class or audience will ask, "Don't you have to tell a lot of lies?"

The correct answer is "No!" and I say it over and over with vehemence. It's never a good idea to lie to the media, no matter how heinous the truth may be. We only have to witness the aftermath of lies told by some of the most famous failures in recent history: Ford Motor Company lying about the safety of the Ford Explorer equipped with Firestone Wilderness Tires; Congressman Anthony Weiner lying about the Twitter posting of a photo displaying his bulging underwear; and President Bill Clinton telling the world that he "did not have sex with that woman." Lying to the media, constituents, and customers leads only to the revelation of the truth, exposing the liar and often ending an otherwise promising career.

That being said, it's easy enough for me to tell you never to lie, but clients will ask you to do so—clients you respect and with whom you enjoy working. I can only offer you this guideline: Telling the truth is never as injurious as lying about it and attempting to cover it up. The truth will come out, either through media investigation, a whistle-blower on the client's staff, a disgruntled former employee, or an activist friendly to the opposing cause. Take it from the story of former congressman Bob Livingstone, "outed" for extramarital affairs on the eve of his election as Speaker of the House of Representatives: The truth will rear its head at the least advantageous and most embarrassing moment. Livingston had no choice but to withdraw, rather than continue to lead the call for President Clinton's impeachment for lying about an extramarital affair.

You may also be asked to tell only part of the truth, keeping certain details out of the public eye. These are situations that must be considered on a case-by-case basis, particularly if withholding the rest of the information will not in any way injure customers or constituents. It may be necessary to explain that a CEO is stepping down for health reasons, for example, but it's not required that the public know the extent of his cancer, his treatment schedule, his doctors' names, or the prognosis.

My advice to you is this: Trust your instincts. If you're an experienced PR professional, you know when a statement or story will not hold water with the media, or when it will fall apart under scrutiny. If you're new to the field, don't be frightened by your lack of experience—your gut will tell you when you're about to do something that feels very wrong. Most of all, be ready to tell the client, "I'm advising you that this is the wrong thing to do, and I must stand by my own principles on this."

Finally, be prepared to push back from the table and walk away. Good clients will see how seriously you mean to extricate yourself from the situation, and will take your advice to stick with the truth. Not-so-good clients will become angry with you and try to make the problem your fault. It's up to you what to do from this point forward, but remember that you work for yourself, and you always have the option of resigning from a situation that will have a negative impact on your business and your career.

Guard against Your Own Errors

It can happen to any of us: The wrong version of a news release goes out to the media, with an unedited quote that strikes the wrong tone for the product launch. Or you're not as sure of a product's features as you thought you were, and you blurt out the wrong answer while you're talking to a reporter. Or worse, you hold a press conference and no media show up. Bad things happen, but in most cases, we can recover and move forward if we deal with them responsibly and professionally.

- **Maintain the paper trail.** Keep every e-mail you receive from a client, every approval or sign-off on a news release, and every client's signature on a graphic layout. If you have all of this documentation, you can prove that you had their permission to use information, distribute a release, or go to press with a printed piece. Their signature indicates that they reviewed the materials. They may still object, but it will be harder for them to blame you for the error or omission.
- **Know when you're wrong, and admit to the error.** If you do make a mistake, take responsibility as quickly as possible. Just as lying won't work with the media, pretending that you are not at fault will not help you keep the client—and trying to blame him or her for your error will most certainly result in your eventual termination.

- **Offer a solution.** Whether or not the error is yours, it's up to you to correct it as quickly as possible. Determine the best course of action and a secondary route if the first one is not effective. It's fairly easy to call up a reporter and say, "Look, I didn't give you good information before, but I have what you need now." It's much harder to retract a statement that's already in print or on the air.

- **Offer a monetary concession.** If you've made a recommendation to a client that turned out to do more harm than good, or if you've made an error that can't be rectified without considerable effort, you may have to swallow your fee. We can't charge clients for our own mistakes or our efforts to correct them. Make sure your client sees the "no charge" line on your invoice, so he or she knows that you've acknowledged your culpability and been fair with your final compensation.

- **Protect yourself from the worst.** It's very rare that a solo public relations practitioner will be placed in a position to make egregious errors that could truly damage a company, but if your specialty is crisis communications or politics or if you handle a lot of confidential information for a large corporation, you may need to carry errors and omissions insurance. This safeguard will protect your home and property by paying a settlement to your client should you find yourself the defendant in a lawsuit. (More about this insurance in chapter 5.)

Client Confidentiality

Some clients require a high level of confidentiality, enough that they will expect you to sign a nondisclosure agreement to work on their business. Take this agreement seriously, and take steps within your workspace to be sure that no one can read any information about this client accidentally—not your family, your cleaning service, your friends stopping by, nor other clients. While this may sound like the tradecraft of espionage, the fact is that you have no way of knowing who may be interested in the information lying on your desk or glowing on your computer screen.

Maintaining confidentiality is fairly easy for home-based businesses, because you receive minimal traffic through your office. With just a few precautions, you can assure your clients that their information is safe with you.

- **Work at home.** Don't take your client's confidential information with you to work on at your favorite coffee shop. Keep it in a controlled space.

- **Put things away.** When you leave your desk for a meeting or at the end of the day, put all of the confidential information away in a file drawer. Don't leave it on your desk.
- **Shred copies of documents.** If you make extra copies for a meeting and you don't distribute them at the client site, don't recycle them. Shred them when you get home.
- **Return reference documents.** When the project is completed or when you have finished using reports, white papers, or other documents provided by your client, return them to the client's place of business. If you need them again, you can always ask for them.
- **Use a password-protected FTP site.** If you and your client pass large documents between you online, use an FTP service that only allows access with a unique password for each user. Assign one password to your client, and make that client's documents available only with that password.
- **Keep these documents out of the cloud.** With the newness of cloud computing, your client may not be comfortable with his documents living "somewhere" on the web. Maintain the option of file storage on your computer for special cases.

The Curse of the Unethical Supplier

As careful as you may be in choosing vendors with whom to do business, you may encounter a situation in which a supplier you've engaged for a project does not share your ethical standards.

I selected a printing company for a client's high-end brochure, a beautiful sixteen-page extravaganza with translucent vellum over the cover. The gorgeous piece would become a highlight of my portfolio for years to come, and I looked forward to delivering five thousand of these booklets to my client.

Two days after the delivery, my client called me in a panic. "There are spots all over the insides of some of these," she said. "I can't distribute them in this condition. We'll have to reprint."

I called the printer, expecting him to move quickly to determine the cause of the problem and to reprint the piece. To my amazement, he immediately blamed the graphic artist for faults in the files he sent to the prepress department. He had never mentioned any issues with these files throughout the pre-production phases, and the press proofs had shown no unsightly spots. I'd done my own print production for many years, so I knew exactly where the problem had developed: on a dirty press.

When I went to the print shop and suggested that he would find the problem there, the printing company owner began to pace and growl. I could see anger building up, and I actually took a couple of steps backward. Sure enough, he began a tirade that went on for some time, all about how expensive and complicated this piece was, and how it was far beyond what his company normally took on, "but I wanted to do it for you, to show you what we could do." He offered no concession and no reprint. He blamed everyone from my client for her upscale taste in graphic design, to me for what he called the "rush" turnaround—a fairly standard three weeks.

When he finally calmed down, I told him that I now had some subset of five thousand pieces I could not use, and I needed to work with him to find a solution. He walked away, saying, "I can't talk to you about this now."

It took me two weeks to negotiate a reprinting. In the meantime, I sat with my client and went through the original five thousand pieces page by page to find the ones that were usable so she could complete her initial mailing. The printer eventually reprinted the rest, delaying the folding and stitching steps over the course of several weeks until we finally received the last delivery. The incident not only ended my relationship with this printer, but also damaged my credibility with the client. It took me another year to earn her trust at the level I had enjoyed before the printer saga.

How could I have avoided such a kerfuffle? This happened before the web became the world's principal source of information, but today, it's easy to use a search engine to find customer references, complaints, and other comments about any merchant. Live references from other customers provide many insights, especially if you can use your interviewing skills in a phone conversation to dig out the details of a lukewarm recommendation.

Whenever you choose a supplier or vendor, your client's experience with this vendor reflects on you and your good judgment. Make these choices carefully to avoid the worst possible scenarios.

10 Marketing Your Business

I'm often contacted by people who are either considering a move into self-employment, or who have already made the leap and are struggling to maintain a profitable level of business. When I meet these folks for lunch or coffee and they ask for my advice, my first question is almost always the same: "What are you doing to market your business?"

Remarkably, the answer is almost always the same as well: "Oh, but I hate selling. I really can't sell myself."

You can probably imagine how I respond to this: "So you're in business for yourself, and you don't want to sell your services. How do you expect to stay in business?"

Owning your own business is all about marketing your services within your market sector and beyond, attending networking events, meeting new people, calling people you've never met, and convincing them that you can make their lives easier and help them reach their goals. Clients will come and go, the economy will rise and fall, and through it all you need to maintain your income so you can pay your bills and fund your retirement.

If you hate selling, you've reached the crossroads in your decision to keep your day job or own your own business. With the understanding that selling your services will be an everyday activity, can you move forward?

Let's assume that you can, so we can start talking about how.

Where to Find Clients

Remember the three-tiered list you created in chapter 6? This gives you a terrific starting point in your quest to sign your first clients. If your list of potential clients (we'll call them *prospects*) feels a little thin to you, you can add lots of names quickly by widening your circle of acquaintances.

From the Field

Elliott Stares, Elliott Stares Public Relations, Inc. (www.esprinc.com)

GLOBAL PERSPECTIVE, LOCAL RESULTS

How can a one-man PR firm land accounts like the Miami Dolphins, Sony Ericsson, Rolex, and Danny DeVito's South Beach restaurant?

When you're Elliott Stares, handling high-profile media relations for top international brands is just another day at the office.

With early training at the London, England, headquarters of Hill & Knowlton (H&K), this British-born PR professional developed a taste for clients in the spotlight very early in his career. "They split my time between the marketing communications divisions of sports marketing and retail," he said, "so I was thrown head first into working for PetSmart, Cadbury-Schweppes, and Walker's Crisps. I worked on Gillette and the pan-European launch of the Mach 3, the first three-blade razor. I worked on the Cricket World Cup, the Rugby World Cup, and the Athens [Greece] bid for the 2004 Olympics." The focused PR campaign H&K ran across Europe has been credited, in part, with Athens' bid win.

Even with such a glamorous series of clients in a top-ten agency, Stares knew he could do more—and he got his first taste of working independently while still employed with H&K. "One of my biggest projects was the first land-speed motorcycle record attempt for Gillette," he said. "They sent me to the US to the salt flats of Utah, and I worked with the rocket scientist who developed the technology to travel at five hundred miles per hour. That was the most prestigious project on which they sent me on my own."

Stares' success record made him particularly attractive to agencies with high-profile accounts, so when a senior H&K executive, Jon Tibbs, moved to a new PR firm, he called on Stares to join him there. "He brought me with him to work on the 2008 Beijing Olympic bid," he said, naming another massive PR victory. "That was a solid six-months campaign, acting as European communications manager, lobbying the IOC. It really gave me the vision of wanting to work in the sports arena."

Continuing to work for Tibbs, but out of his own flat in northwest London, Stares began work for a client who planned to establish a European-style soccer academy in Miami, Florida. "I came over to Miami in 2001 and worked out of a hotel, and started forming relationships with the local media," he said. "For the launch of CareerSports Soccer Academy, we had every local TV crew and every local sports journalist, we had UK soccer star Ray Hudson, and [Colombian soccer player] Carlos Valderrama. It was a tremendous success."

The soccer academy closed less than a year later, but by this time, Stares had fallen in love with south Florida. "I had burnt myself out in London—it was very high intensity there," he said. "I wanted to start fresh, where no one knew me. I fell in love with the weather, and I'd formed relationships in south Florida."

Starting off with a single client—the creator of DanceStar USA, the American Dance Music Awards—Stares got to know national and international media in the entertainment and music worlds while working out of DanceStar's downtown Miami office. "I started to form other relationships in Miami as people saw the results I could generate," he said. "They wanted me to start working with them. So I started to bring on my own business as an individual PR consultant."

Stares left DanceStar and partnered for several years with the boutique PR firm Tara, Ink, but the press of his own business opportunities became too great. Making the break in 2008, he took on the nationwide launch of Zalia Cosmetics, the first line of cosmetics designed for Latino women. "That really gave me the confidence I needed to continue with my own consultancy," he said. "I started winning other pieces of business in various industry sectors. I launched the first telenovela acting school in Miami, I worked with Remix Hotel Miami, and I started winning business with Sony Ericsson and other blue chip companies that wanted to reach the Miami music and entertainment market."

From a mobile phone and a laptop, with a desk in his Miami Beach apartment as his base of operations, Stares now serves as the US media relations representative for the Rolex brand's entertainment sports promotions, FIFA Beach Soccer (the international soccer federation), entertainment coverage for the Miami Dolphins, and the Miami Beach Polo World Cup, among others. "Some of the best people in the business are independent," he said. "I've seen the client's frustration with meeting the agency head and never seeing that person again. When you assign the fate of a client to a team, it does not always bring the type of results that you can generate on your own. It's me, the owner of the agency, who's stuffing every press kit, pitching every story, and attending every media event. That's how I can get the results for my clients."

Widen Your Network

If your A list is shorter than you would like, you need to meet more people who have the decision-making ability to select you as their public relations service provider.

How do you do this? Get out and mingle with the masses in your target field.

- Attend **trade shows** in your market niche to meet people in your industry from all over the country—or even from around the world. Make the most of trade shows by attending seminars, walking the show floor, and getting invited to as many cocktail parties and hospitality suite events as you can schedule.

- Go to **educational conferences** in your field. If you're a good public speaker, offer to lead a seminar at the conference on smart public relations for people in this industry. Show off your expertise while you position yourself as an expert in your field—which, of course, you are.

- Go to **professional association** events in your own geographic area. Network with people who work in your target market at mixers and monthly meetings. Serve on a committee—especially the marketing or communications committee—to form working relationships with other committee members, and to show off your own skill.

- Join the **Public Relations Society of America chapter in your area** to meet PR managers from all kinds of companies in your geographic market. Most chapters would love the offer of a presentation at a monthly meeting, covering some aspect of PR in which you have considerable expertise. People interested in your topic will attend the presentation, and you may find yourself the recipient of several business cards from people who could use your services.

- Serve on a **nonprofit board** in your area. Be careful to choose an organization about which you have a real passion for the cause! Nonprofit boards can be labor intensive, especially if you plan to serve on committees to demonstrate your PR prowess. If you sit on a board just because someone offered you a seat, you will come to resent the time you take away from your business to perform your duties. When you bring passion to the job, however, your skills will shine and attract the right kind of attention.

- Attend **nonprofit fundraising events** for causes that relate to your field of specialization. For example, if you are targeting medical professionals and hospitals as potential clients, attend fundraisers for the American Cancer Society and the American Diabetes Association, to name just a couple of the many charities in this sector. If you want to reach companies in the ever-growing environmental market, look for events for your local land trust, Nature Conservancy chapter, Sierra Club, Audubon Society, and others in this segment.

Remember that growing your business is all about balance: doing an exemplary job for clients while working to bring in new clients, all while keeping your daily billable hours at the level you require. Find the best possible blend of working at home and attending outside events, with the understanding that the client's immediate needs must come first. You may want to limit your networking schedule to one event per week, or three per month, to maintain the balance that allows you to apply your most productive hours to your clients' projects.

Use LinkedIn

LinkedIn, the premier networking site for businesspeople, offers excellent opportunities to ask friends and associates for introductions to people you would like to know. Once you've created your LinkedIn profile page (more on that later in this chapter), begin by linking to people you know now—colleagues, former clients, classmates from your high school and college, and friends. Every time you link to someone new, go to their profile page and take a few minutes to peruse their contact lists. Chances are excellent that you will find a name or two that resonates with you, a person who works for a company you'd like to approach for business.

When you find these names, send a message to your connections, explain that you have started your own PR business, and ask if they would be willing to introduce you to these people in their connections lists. The introduction could be as simple as an e-mail to their connection with a copy to you, giving you the prospect's e-mail address so you can follow up in the near future.

Some of your connections may say no to your request. They may not feel that they know you or your target prospect well enough to recommend you, or even to make a basic introduction. It's their right to turn you down, but don't be discouraged—there are plenty of other potential prospects out there, and lots of people who will be more willing to help you make the initial connection.

Ask the Editors

Editors of trade magazines often get inquiries from advertisers who need a PR professional who understands their market. As you build relationships with editors in the vertical markets in which you specialize, they will come to know your skills and your ability to bring them usable material. Once they know you well, ask them for referrals to other companies in their market sector who could make good use of your services. I've had some of my best and most profitable referrals come from editors who respect my work in their specialized field.

Referrals from the Big Agencies

Many large advertising and public relations agencies receive inquiries from businesses and organizations who do not offer enough income potential to warrant their taking them on as clients. For your firm, however, these clients are exactly the right size. You can enjoy a steady stream of referrals from these agencies when you cement a referring relationship with them, giving them the easy "out" they need to pass on the business gracefully, with the knowledge that the client will receive top-notch service from you.

Get these agencies' attention by reaching out to the decision-makers in the public relations division. A clever mailing piece or a three-dimensional gift (edible gifts are always well received), followed by an offer to stop by for a brief introduction, can help you begin a mutually beneficial relationship that lasts for many years.

Profit Booster: Thank-You Gifts

Would you like to be at the top of the list for all the people who might refer business your way? Give a gift for every referral that turns into paying business for you. A cookie bouquet, a box of locally made chocolates, or a basket of muffins can leave a lasting impression with the person who made the referral. Next time they meet someone who's looking for public relations assistance, your name will be the first that comes to mind.

Reaching Prospects

You've built a great list of potential clients, but how will you get their attention, make first contact, and get meetings with them on your calendar?

Most public relations professionals have some experience with the marketing side of the communication coin. It's time to pull out all the things you know and use them for your own benefit! Here are some of the tools at your disposal to help you reach the right people with the right message.

Direct Marketing

Thanks to the comprehensive nature of the web, we no longer need to create lengthy, expensive capabilities brochures that detail every aspect of our business, and send them out in fancy envelopes at today's inflated postage prices. Instead, your direct marketing can be simple, to the point, and even fun, sparking prospects' interest enough so they remember the piece when you call them by phone a few days after they receive it.

Even in this digital world, the basic rules of marketing continue to apply:

- Your direct marketing piece should not be lengthy, but it must be both informative and memorable.
- Whether you send your marketing pieces by US mail, as PDFs in e-mails, or in some combination of the two, the pieces need to look like they've come from the same company and are part of a cohesive campaign. This will help you build name recognition.
- Use humor very carefully, and vet your humorous copy with colleagues who will give you an objective opinion. Humor can be a very personal thing—not everyone agrees on what's funny and what isn't. Above all, avoid politics, religion, race, or gender issues in making your joke.
- Repeat impressions are more effective than a single impression. Think in terms of a campaign, and send a series of at least three pieces (by mail or e-mail) to build recognition of your name and message.
- If you're sending a series of flyers by e-mail, give your prospect an easy way to opt out. This may mean that someone you really want to reach will use this sterile way to reject your approach, but it's better to have her do that than to let her feel that you're spamming her.

- Take the time to send your e-mails individually to each person, rather than blind-copying them to a large list. E-mails that are not addressed directly to the recipient can land in corporate spam filters, negating the value of your efforts.
- Always back up your literature or e-mails with a phone call. Don't wait for the world to beat a path to your door; it's up to you to make the initial voice-to-voice contact to break the ice with your prospect.
- If you've called three times, left voicemail, and never made live contact with your prospect, give it a rest for a few weeks, at least, before trying again.

Introductory Gifts

In my first week in business, I took the first twelve people on my A list of prospects and sent them each a live, potted, purple violet plant and a card, letting them know that Minetor & Company (with its purple logo) was now live and operational. Several of them called me when they received the plant, and others readily took my call when I followed up by phone a few days later.

To my amazement, I had signed seven of these people as clients by the end of the following week.

My results were not typical, but they do indicate the fertile ground your A list can provide. Make your best and most memorable approach to these people at the outset, and you may find yourself with a strong client roster before you can say "seasonal fruit basket."

Gifts of tangible value—edible, living (as in plants, not animals), and practical (like a flash drive imprinted with your new logo)—are some of the best door openers

Thinkpoint: Market at a Reasonable Pace

You are the only person on your sales force, so don't overwhelm yourself and your resources with mass mailings to a hundred prospects at a time. Start with a dozen, and work your way down the list. If your efforts result in all the clients you can handle for the time being, ease off on the marketing—but don't turn it off completely. Approach just one or two prospects a week while your plate is full, to be sure that you'll continue to have plenty of business when the current projects come to a close.

you can buy. Perhaps a local candy company can recreate your logo in solid chocolate. A jar of M&M candies in your corporate colors will bring a smile to a prospect's face. Any item that makes your prospect's day a little bit easier—especially if it's fun and high-tech—will make him think of you the next time a rush job crosses his desk. If your name evokes a clever play on words, go for the humor (you're sharing a laugh about yourself, which is always appropriate).

Showcase Your Expertise

Your direct marketing efforts reach people whom you already know may be looking for the services you can provide. To reach beyond these people to the vast market of businesses that are not on your list, seed the web with demonstrations of your expertise.

- **An online column on a trade magazine's website** gives you the tacit imprimatur of that magazine's editorial staff, making you a bona fide expert. Write about issues in communications for your target market, bringing them insights on a wide range of PR-related topics.
- **Comment intelligently** on articles others have written, with a link to your website in your signature.
- Offer to **lead and assemble a panel** at a trade show that reaches your target market, positioning yourself as a leader in revealing communications or media issues your prospects may face.
- **Make presentations at professional associations**—both in your home geographic area and in other cities, if that's appropriate for your business—about public relations messages and challenges in the vertical markets you serve.
- **Start a blog** and keep it active, posting your insights about public relations in general and issues clients like yours regularly face. Once you start a blog, post a new entry at least every two weeks, and more often if you can do it. As you develop a fan base, they will keep visiting to see what new insights you offer.
- **Work the media.** This is what you do best! Get your name in the magazines and on the websites your prospects read. Make yourself the go-to person in your industry for image management questions about high-profile people, companies, and topics.

Keep Your Website Current

We talked at length about creating your website in chapter 5, but the story only begins with the site's launch. Make the commitment to updating your website regularly, posting the results of completed projects, and providing all the information a prospect needs to click "Contact Us" and send you an e-mail requesting a meeting.

As your business grows and your roster of successes grows with it, make posting your success story a part of every project's conclusion. Write a short, newsy description of the project's objectives and the steps you took to reach the client's goals. Ask your client for a testimonial quote that you can put on the project's page, and see if the editors or producers who provided coverage of the story will give you a quote as well. Add a PDF of a finished press kit or printed pieces, photos of an event, or other visuals that represent the deliverables for this job, and you've got a new web page you can upload to your site in a jiffy.

In addition to news about your business, draw more attention to your site by providing sticky content—things that change regularly enough that they draw people back again and again. For example, many news sites offer RSS feeds—for Really Simple Syndication—that allow you to display a rolling news feed on your site with headlines of articles that relate to your market. If you write a column on a professional association site, you can add the RSS feed for your column to a page on your website as well. When people visit your site, they can simply click on the headline that interests them and go directly to this article.

Other sticky content can include a Quote of the Day feature, a daily blog post, quizzes or contests, product giveaways, or updates about your clients' activities or business—especially if your clients include celebrities, travel destinations, restaurants, or other people or places about which readers seek information regularly.

There's nothing worse than a prospect landing on your website and discovering that it's months or even years out of date. Make the commitment to update it regularly, and you will see results in the number of hits you receive.

Create a Facebook Page

With more than 700 million users as of this writing, Facebook has become the go-to place for anybody who lives, breathes, and types with their thumbs. Your clients will expect you to incorporate Facebook into their communications initiatives, so your business page on the site can demonstrate your savvy in working with this still-new PR tool.

Facebook makes it extraordinarily easy to set up a page for your business. Make this distinctly different from the page you use to keep in touch with friends and family, as its use will be more professionally friendly than your personal page. You may have seen other business pages with lots of graphics, designed tabs, and other elements, but none of these are necessary—what's important on Facebook is content, and the conversation you maintain with people who "like" your page.

As Facebook changes its format and adds functionality fairly regularly, check the Help Center to find out how to set up a business account in the current format. Once you've set up the account, you'll go directly to the "Get Started" page. Here you can upload an image (probably your logo or professional head shot), fill out the Info page with relevant information about your business, and invite your friends and business associates to Like your page. Keep in touch with your followers by posting interesting content. The messages you post will show up in the news feed of all of your page's fans.

So . . . what's interesting content? I'm going to assume for the moment that you are already a Facebook user, and that you've become a fan of at least a couple of pages for products, books, or celebrities you like. Do you look for the posts from these pages that appear in your news feed? What kinds of things catch your eye? You already know the answer to this: news you can use, fun facts, great photos, interesting quotes, quizzes and contests, and every once in a while, an actual sales message. Remember that Facebook is a place for creating relationships through conversation, and people don't take kindly to advertising. Talk *with* your fans, not at them—and tell them something that will make them stop and look for more than a second or two. Did you come across a fascinating factoid today while researching a client's topic? Did you read a funny story in a trade magazine that you can share on your page, with a link to the story on the journal's website? Is a client sending you to a trade show, where you can "report" by posting from the show floor? There's no end to the content you can provide. .

When you have their attention, you will know it: The number of people who like your page will grow, and you'll start to see people respond to your posts by clicking the Like button on the post itself. If you've had your Facebook page for a month or so and you're not seeing the response you want, change up the content with something you haven't tried before. Holding your audience's interest is the key to success.

You may be wondering what all of this Facebook activity actually does for you. That's a good, relevant question. Facebook gives you the opportunity to position yourself as an expert in your field, one who keeps an eye on this market niche and knows what's going on within your area(s) of expertise, what's on the leading edge, and what comes next. Best of all, you can do this without having to write long expertise articles or publish a book to prove that you're a maven in your industry. All you have to do is post a quick status update two or three times a week, which won't take you more than a minute or two to do.

Create a LinkedIn Profile

LinkedIn, the bastion of the upwardly mobile, the unemployed, and the employed-but-considering-my-options, presents a completely different picture from your Facebook business page. This networking site is all business and yet very personal, a place for you to post the particulars of your curriculum vitae for others to peruse when they are looking for the right PR person to hire.

As such, your LinkedIn profile must be thorough, polished, and succinct, a resume and references that live online for the long term. In today's business climate, a LinkedIn profile is not optional, but making the most of it is an option that most employed people do not embrace.

It's up to you as an individual and as a business owner to build your profile, link to a long list of contacts, and keep your page fresh so it can work hard for you. Like your website, your LinkedIn page is out there when you're not paying attention, suggesting to prospects that they may benefit from a working relationship with you.

It takes about a minute to set up a LinkedIn account, but it will take some time to build your profile. Treat this with the seriousness you apply to your resumé, but with an emphasis on the long form—on LinkedIn, more information is better. Fill out the Summary portion with a solid description of your skills and experience, using the same kinds of persuasive techniques you would use if you were writing for a client. This is not the place for self-deprecating modesty; the people who view your profile are looking for the public relations professional they need to solve an issue for them, or to become the perfect outsource for their overworked communications department.

Once you have your profile in place, start collecting connections by searching on the names of people you know. LinkedIn will allow you to connect to just about anyone, so long as you already have some acquaintance with these people. Each time you click the "Add NAME to your network" button, a window appears that asks how you know NAME: as a colleague, classmate, someone you've done business with, friend, or "other." If you choose "other," the system asks you to enter NAME's e-mail address—and if the address you enter does not match the one LinkedIn has on file for that person, your connection request will be blocked.

You also have the option of saying that you don't know NAME, but you will be blocked from connecting with NAME if you choose this answer.

This level of privacy and security makes LinkedIn the preferred business networking tool. You'll never be flooded with resumés from recent college graduates looking for their first job, and strangers who want information (i.e., free) interviews with you cannot hound you. By the same token, on LinkedIn you can only reach out to people you already know. When you're getting started in your own business, LinkedIn offers the most cost-effective way to track down and reconnect with long-lost clients, former colleagues, and others who know your work and respect your capabilities.

Once you've made some connections, LinkedIn will begin offering you additional people with whom you might want to connect, based on the number of connections you have in common. You'll begin to see names pop up that you had not even considered in your list of potential clients—and some of these may be interested in hearing the news of your at-home business.

As you connect with these people from your professional past and present, ask them to help you complete your profile by posting a recommendation of your work. This may feel like you're fishing for compliments—something that goes against the grain for a lot of us—but your list of recommendations can be a powerful tool in turning a potential client's attention toward you. Even if a non-competition agreement forbids you from soliciting your former clients for work, they can still serve as solid references, and many will be happy to do so.

When you've got a nice list of comments about your work, provide a link to your LinkedIn profile on your website, either from the home page or from the page with your biographical information.

LinkedIn offers a number of paid services to help you connect with people beyond those you already know. If your initial contact list does not net you the roster of clients you need to support you and your household, you may want to explore these services and upgrade your membership.

To Tweet or Not to Tweet?

One of the most common questions my clients ask me is about Twitter, and the need to send 140-character messages out on a regular basis—several times a day or more—on any number of topics. Does this practice bring value to every business regardless of its products or services, or is it really only effective for celebrities?

There's no simple answer to this question, so let's explore it for a moment.

If you're not already Twittering, here's what it's about. Twitter is a social networking site on which you can create a brief profile—a 140-character description of yourself—and start posting messages (called tweets) from your smartphone or computer whenever the spirit moves you to do so. To be effective, you must build a strong list of followers, so someone is actually reading your tweets.

Twitter differs significantly from Facebook in that you don't need to know the people you follow personally, and you don't need their permission to follow them. You may want to start with your friends and acquaintances, but you can branch out beyond your usual circle to people who share your interests and tweet about things you want to read. Here's the beauty of the system: Most of the people you choose to follow will follow you back. Soon you'll have a big list of followers.

Then what? Just as you fill your Facebook page with newsy stuff, do the same on Twitter. If there's a great PR gaffe in the media this week, tweet about it and tell your followers how it could have been handled better (always in bites of 140 characters or less). If your area of specialization is hotels and tourism, tweet about specials your clients offer, or about the exciting new amenities travelers will find in hotels on their next vacation. News in your field, things you've just read, links to interesting facts and articles, a terrific new website with tips . . . any of these things and thousands more make for fast and easy tweeting. Of course, your clients' events and news releases make excellent tweets as well.

Like all social networking tools, Twitter can take on a life of its own, dominating your thoughts as you worry about what to tweet next. It's up to you to determine what kind of commitment to tweeting will be productive for you, and to monitor your own Twitter habit to keep it from dominating your working life. Not every business benefits from an active Twitter feed. This is one tool in an ever-growing chest of social networking options, so give it its rightful, moderated place in your business day.

Promotion through Business Classification

If you're a minority or female business owner, avenues may be open to you in your state to register your business as minority owned. Many large corporations and government agencies look for opportunities to contract with businesses owned by women and minorities, so your registration—promoted on your website and on your business cards—may garner you some introductions that might not find their way to you otherwise.

If your business operates in the middle of a large city, your downtown location may also work in your favor. Many governments offer grants and growth opportunities to businesses in challenged areas, or in neighborhoods targeted for revitalization. In particular, the US Small Business Administration (SBA) offers certification for businesses in HUBZones, or Historically Underutilized Business Zones in urban and rural communities. Businesses that are certified gain "preferential access to federal procurement opportunities," according to the SBA website.

The SBA also runs the Women-Owned Small Business Federal Contract Program, which sets aside certain federal contracts for eligible women-owned small businesses or economically disadvantaged women-owned small businesses. To be eligible, your firm must be owned at least 51 percent by a woman, and managed by a woman who is a US citizen.

If you are Native American, the Indian Affairs' Division of Economic Development can certify your business as a Native American Minority-Owned Business, which makes you eligible for a number of services to help your business grow.

You can explore these and other options on the SBA website at www.sba.gov.

To be certified as a Minority-Owned Business, your firm must be at least 51 percent owned by someone who is Asian, African-American, Hispanic, or Native American. The National Minority Supplier Development Council handles this certification, which makes your business eligible for government contracts that have been set aside by law for minority-owned businesses. More information on this program is available at the Minority and Women Business Enterprises website at www.mwbe.com.

11

Building Client Relationships

Bringing in new clients takes work, and lots of it. Once you've secured a relationship with a client, making that client as happy as he can be becomes the number one priority—because it's easier, cheaper, and far more pleasurable to expand the business you do with your current clients than it is to go out, start from scratch, and find new ones.

Ten Things Clients Love

What makes clients love their public relations firm? Here's a top ten list (in no special order).

1. **Conference reports.** A quick but detailed recap of the gist of a meeting, the action items and who's responsible for them, and a timeline for the project's progress can do wonders for keeping a project on track. Your clients will thank you for this basic bit of account management.
2. **Keeping your word.** If you say the release will be finished on Tuesday, make sure it's on the client's desk on Tuesday, if not before. Make only the promises you can keep, set expectations accordingly, and do the things you say you will do.
3. **Intelligent questions.** Never be afraid to ask a question, even if it seems off the wall or if you're afraid it will reveal your ignorance of a topic. The questions you think are foolish may actually penetrate to the heart of the flaw in the message.
4. **Prompt responses.** Everyone understands that you may be in a meeting or on a conference call when a client phones or texts you, but that client wants a response in a timely manner. Return the call, text, or e-mail at your first opportunity, whether or not you feel like

doing so. What you fear will be a lengthy discussion may turn out to be a quick question.

5. **Follow up before they do.** When you're in the midst of an ongoing project, keep the client informed of your progress. Don't wait for him to call to ask; make sure he knows you're moving forward or that you've hit an obstacle and need his assistance to sort it out.

6. **Client management.** Sometimes a client needs a little gentle prodding to send you the information you need or to connect you with an internal source whose calendar you need to access. Busy clients often let things slide without meaning to do so, and they appreciate the cheerful nudge that keeps them on track.

7. **When you're smarter than they are.** Clients hire you for your expertise, so never be afraid to speak up when you see them heading in the wrong direction. Don't just do what they say when you know it's a bad course of action. The caveats and watch-outs you offer can save them time, money, and embarrassment.

8. **Thinking about them when you don't have to.** When you're reading through the morning headlines and you see a story about your client's competitor, or about a topic that you know interests her, send her a link to the story to be sure she sees it as well. You may not be on retainer, but the fact that you thought of her when she wasn't paying you to do so will leave a positive impression.

9. **A memory for details.** When your client needs to know which advertising specialties supplier printed his trade show premiums five years ago, be there with that information. Later, when you're at the trade show, be the person who can remind the client which editors gave him what coverage, so he can mention it to them at happy hour. If you can then remember where he left his briefcase, you will be his hero.

10. **Saving their butts.** Someone you interviewed for a news release calls your client in a fury when the piece runs in a newspaper, claiming he never saw the final draft and didn't say all of those things. Luckily, you not only made sure the source saw the draft before it went out to the media, but you also kept all the documentation and his e-mail with his final approval. Nothing can make your client happier than that.

Ten Things Clients Hate

Want to know how to lose a client in ten easy steps? Here are the moves that will make your client escort you to the door.

1. **Surprises.** So you're scheduled to deliver the drafts of the press kit copy on Wednesday, but you can see it's not going to be possible because of issues with the people you have to interview, the sheer volume of writing, or the other projects passing through at the same time. If you wait until Wednesday to tell your client, she can't set the expectations for her higher-ups who are expecting copy on their desks. Always discuss a slipping timeline, obstacles to completion, and any other issues as soon as they arise.

2. **Questions you didn't ask.** You don't understand some aspect of your client's business, but you fear that you look like an idiot, so you stop asking. Don't worry, you'll look much more foolish later when that lack of comprehension comes through in the news release you write. If you don't get it, say so. It may be that the person explaining the concept is not very good at doing so—cut through the jargon and the technical language and ask for an explanation in plain English. I ran into this with an engineer who had designed lenses for the giant Keck Telescope, who did not realize that I had never taken physics and didn't have the basic knowledge to understand light refraction. Once he understood why I was mystified, he had no trouble helping me see the light.

3. **Nickel-and-dime charges.** A client asks you to copy his press kit to a single CD to take with him to a meeting. You do so, and charge him $5 for this on your next invoice. Worse, you take a client to lunch, and then the cost of the lunch shows up when you bill him for the project. These may be common practices at large agencies, but they are extraordinarily irritating to clients, and frankly, they're classless.

4. **Lies.** This probably requires no explanation. Once you're caught in a lie, you will not only lose the client, but you sacrifice your reputation as a straight shooter as well. Remember that no client is an island; they will talk to others and tell the story of your lack of honesty. Lying is an endgame for putting yourself out of business.

5. **Inflated expectations.** Overpromising and under-delivering—what are you, a used car salesman? Don't tell your client that his story will be on the front page of the *Wall Street Journal* if you can't get it there.

6. **The blame game.** If you hire a vendor and that vendor delivers substandard work, blaming the vendor will not get you out of a sticky situation. You chose the vendor, which makes the problem your responsibility to solve. The same goes for internal people at your client's place of business—if someone stiffs you for an interview and you can't finish the project without it, don't point fingers. You'll be amazed at how quickly a client's company will circle the wagons to protect the person you've blamed for the problem! Instead, alert your client to the delay and ask if there's another way to get the information.

7. **The end-run (around your client to his boss).** It can be very tempting to just go over your client's head to her boss to get a job done, but nothing good ever comes of doing so. You'll break your unspoken covenant to work in partnership with your client, and you may never be able to regain that trust.

8. **Becoming suddenly unavailable.** You decide that you really need a mental health day, but your client is expecting to hear from you. You're in business for yourself, so he has no one else he can call for the information he needs. Like it or not, you need to take that call and deal with whatever situation arises. If you drop off the grid without warning, especially in the middle of a crunch project, you can expect your client to start looking for a more dependable supplier.

9. **Pretending to know their business.** There's nothing worse than a PR practitioner who waltzes into a client's office for the first time and tells her everything that's wrong with what she's doing for publicity, and how working with this agency is going to make everything right for her. How can you possibly know? Learn the client's business before you begin to advise her, so you can discover the underlying issues that may not be obvious.

10. **Pretending to "know what they need."** Early in my career, when I was a young account executive, a lazy creative director insisted that I present the lamest piece of artwork I'd ever seen to a client whom I knew would hate it. When I protested, telling him that the piece was completely off base, the creative director darkened and said, "You don't understand. It's what they need!" Sure enough, the client hated it and refused to pay for the agency's creative services. To this day I don't know what was meant by "what they need," but trying to pass off bad work as brilliant strategy will never fly with a smart client.

If you practice exemplary customer service, work to learn the client's business as completely as you can, and maintain your high standards for honesty and integrity in your business dealings, you can avoid all ten of these traps.

How to Take a Vacation

It's easy to believe that once you go into business for yourself, you'll never take another vacation—but it can and must be done, and it's not as hard as it may appear to get the time off. With careful planning, advance communication, and a willingness to keep in touch through all of the wonderful electronic means available to us, you can go off for a much-needed break with the blessings of all of your clients.

I'd been in business eight years when I formed a relationship with Globe Pequot Press that resulted in my writing twenty-one travel-related books over the course of five years. In one year, I actually racked up fourteen weeks of travel, much of it to remote areas in my coverage of America's national parks. Had I let my business slide during those amazing trips, I would have had nothing to come back to when the assignments came to a close—so I developed a solid system for serving my clients from some fairly unusual places. Best of all, I had all the fun of traveling with my photographer husband through some of the most spectacular places in America. Here's how I did it:

First, tell your clients at least three weeks in advance that you're planning to take a week or two off. Send out an e-mail to all of your clients with your date of departure and the date on which you will be back in the office. Use this line: "If there's anything coming up that I can complete for you in advance of my departure, I will be happy to take care of it for you." This usually results in a bit of a business bonanza for the next several weeks.

Let clients know how often you will check your e-mail and your messages, and on what days you will not do so. If you're spending one day or your entire vacation on a tropical island with no mobile phone service, 4G, or Wi-Fi, it's critical that your clients know this. Most clients are decent folk who understand that you need a vacation like anyone else, but some are workaholics who will expect you to be in touch around the clock. Set the expectation of which days you cannot receive calls or retrieve messages.

If you know that a client will need someone with feet on the ground during your absence, arrange with another solo practitioner to cover for you (and do the same for him when he goes on vacation). Bring this person with you to your last client meeting before you go, so your client will know who he is and will not be shy about calling if something needs to be done.

When you are in range, check your voicemail and e-mail and return calls first thing in the morning. Don't wait to check your messages until evening, when you can't reach people to resolve issues. You don't want some nasty message you pick up at 10:00 p.m. to ruin your night's sleep, when you can listen to it and resolve a misunderstanding in minutes in the morning.

Finally, check in with your clients in the morning on the day you return to your office. Let them know you're back home and raring to go, even if you're feeling the post-vacation doldrums. You will find that they have not deserted you for another supplier because you dared to take a week off, and this realization will be enough to buoy you for the busy days ahead.

12

Sweet Success

On that bright, beautiful day when you realize that you have more work than you can handle and lots of opportunities for more, it may be time to think about moving your business out of your home, hiring employees, and planning for significant growth.

Or not.

Many home-based businesses grow to become much larger companies, and just as many never make the leap—not because they don't have the option of doing so, but because working at home offers all the benefits the owner wants. When the time comes for you to decide to go big or stay home, consider your next move carefully. Each option carries its own advantages and disadvantages.

Growth: Pros and Cons

Pros:

- You can take in more business, thus making more money.
- Employees share the workload.
- Employees can cover for you when you're out of the office.
- You can expand your capabilities by hiring people with skills you don't have.
- You can hire support staff to handle clerical tasks you've been doing yourself.
- If you've been lonely as a sole proprietor, having employees will alleviate this issue.
- Moving the business out of your home creates a clear line of demarcation between your work life and your home life.

- You have the option of grooming someone to take over the business when you retire.
- In lieu of that, you have a business you can sell when you're ready to retire.

Cons:

- Being an employer means paying more self-employment taxes: double the SSI and Medicare for each employee.
- You will be required to carry workers' compensation insurance, and you will pay into the state unemployment insurance fund.
- You may be required to offer your employees health insurance, the cost of which will fall in part to you.
- To attract the best employees, you may need to offer retirement savings benefits as well, with contributions that come from your business.
- You become responsible for your employees' income, so you will have to ratchet up your sales activity to be sure your business can support these people.
- Supervising employees can erode your own productivity significantly, as you will have many interruptions and issues to settle between employees. You also have the primary responsibility for training your people.
- If you lose a major client, you may be faced with the need to lay off employees, a miserable task at best.
- You will have the additional costs of leasing office space, buying office furniture and equipment for each employee, utilities, parking, commuting to work, and other expenses associated with a place of business.

With all of this in mind, your business may indeed require this kind of growth. Rather than leaping into a posh office and an extended staff, however, you may find it more cost-effective (and a little less risky) to take small steps toward becoming the next big agency in your area.

The first place to look for office space is in your own home. Do you have additional rooms that can be turned into offices for your first new employees? Or can your current space be modified to provide room for another desk or two as you test your company's potential for growth? Many a large agency has grown from a living/dining room office suite, or from a duplex home in which one side is the residence, while the other is easily remodeled into office space.

If your home office will not allow for this expansion, it may be time to look for space outside your home. Be prepared for the significant leasing expense, especially if you want to be in a tony, upscale area of your city.

When the space-by-the-foot price tag makes you gasp for air, check with your local chamber of commerce to see if new business incubator space is available in your community. These are often former warehouses converted into bare-bones offices, designed to provide new businesses with low-cost space in which they can work and see clients. The space won't be luxurious, but such buildings often have a cutting-edge feel to them that attracts young professionals and stimulates creative thinking. You may have the option of sharing a conference room, Internet connectivity costs, and utilities with another professional services firm across the hall, lowering your cost even further.

Cashing Out

It may be hard to imagine now, but at some point in the future you will want to retire from your business, even if you love it as much when you're in your late sixties as you do today.

As a one-person, home-based business, your retirement savings become your sole responsibility. In your business's first year, make a point of establishing a retirement account to which you and your business can contribute on a monthly or annual basis. Here are two options that are available to you.

1. **The Small Business Owner 401(k):** If the owners of your business (you and a partner, for example) are the only ones eligible to participate in your company's retirement plan, you can open this special 401(k). You can make a salary-deferral contribution of up to 100 percent of your income, but no more than the IRS-allowed salary deferral limit for the year. (In 2012, this limit was $17,000.) Your business can then contribute matching funds of up to 25 percent of your annual salary, but no more than the IRS-allowed limit for that year ($50,000 in 2010).

2. **The Simplified Employee Pension Plan (SEP-IRA):** This Individual Retirement Account (IRA) allows you to contribute up to 25 percent of your income directly to the SEP-IRA, up to an IRS-allowed limit ($49,000 in 2011). Once you make your contribution, you can't withdraw it until you're 59½—and if you wait until you're 70½, withdrawal becomes mandatory.

In addition, you can have a personal IRA or Roth IRA to which you contribute from your salary. Talk to your accountant or financial planner to determine which plan is right for you.

Can You Sell?

How do you sell your home-based business? It's tricky for a one-person shop, because your business depends entirely on your own skills, relationships, and personality for its income. You have a set of clients who have contracted with you to handle their public relations, but there's no guarantee that these clients will stay with the business once you sell it to someone else.

With this in mind, seeking a buyer can be difficult. Begin the process by estimating your firm's value through a business evaluation.

1. **Client analysis.** Which clients are likely to continue to do business with a new owner, and which will fall by the wayside? List all of your clients, your annual income from each, and their method of payment (by the project, on retainer, or end-of-month billing for time spent). If the business continues, how much income can a new owner expect from each?

2. **Vendor analysis.** From whom do you purchase services on a regular basis? Look at your letters of agreement with these vendors and see if there's anything written that prohibits you from transferring your firm's relationship with these suppliers to a new owner. A buyer will see value in maintaining existing relationships with people who know your clients and your business.

3. **Your assets.** Essentially, your business owns some office furniture and equipment, and perhaps some reference materials and supplies. Make a list of these assets, their age, and the likely timetable for replacement. In addition, look at your intangible assets—the value of your brand name, for example—and see if you can place a value on this. You may need to enlist your accountant's help to determine a plausible value.

Now add it all up. This will give you some idea of the value of your business, now and in the future. Review your estimated value with your accountant to see if you've made an accurate assessment.

Can you find a buyer at this price? Some potential prospects include your closest competitors in your market sector or geographic area, including larger agencies that may have an interest in your client list.

If selling your business is not a viable exit strategy, you may want to look at transferring ownership to a younger family member, or simply dissolving the company when you retire. Your attorney can help you choose the right option and take you through all the legal steps necessary to complete your transition.

A Final Word

As I write this, I am well into my fourteenth year as a home-based public relations business owner, and I have never wished I'd stayed in my old job, even though the pay came regularly every two weeks and the benefits were uncommonly generous.

I have survived two major recessions, clients going out of business, clients selling their businesses to new owners who didn't require my services, clients whose scruples were wound in the wrong direction, slow seasons, crunch seasons, and even a year of crushing debt. I have also enjoyed years of prosperity, the flexibility to write twenty-one books in between client projects, travel to forty-seven states, and experiences of absolute joy when my clients achieve successes in which I played some small role.

Some days are not easy, but I have never once looked back longingly at the job with the golden handcuffs that I left behind. If you're like me, and you know that you can succeed by making the break and starting your own business, then I wish you great triumphs and great rewards—and I hope you will let me know how it goes at randi@minetor.com!

Appendix: Web Resources and Organizations

Business Resources on the Web

US Small Business Administration (www.sba.gov): An excellent source for business structure and loan information, and tools for small business growth

Internal Revenue Service (www.irs.gov)

National Association of Woman Business Owners (www.nawbo.org)

Public Relations Society of America (www.prsa.org): The national professional association for PR practitioners

PR News on the Web

Bill Stoller's Publicity Insider (www.publicityinsider.com): Newsletter and website with lots of PR tips and insights

Bulldog Reporter (www.bulldogreporter.com): News, buzz, analysis, profiles of the latest top campaigns, and opinion on PR events, strategies, and tactics

Cision Resource Center (http://us.cision.com/resources/resources_overview.asp): White papers, tip sheets, case studies, articles, webinars, and other information

#journchat: Follow @PRsarahevans on Twitter for this weekly chat that unites journalists and PR people on a variety of topics.

Market Wire Knowledge Sharing (www.MarketWire.com/knowledge_sharing/): A good source for information on communications trends and tactics

PR Leads (www.prleads.com): A subscriptions service for leads on journalists

PR News (www.prnewsonline.com): News site for the latest headlines, insights, and strategies

PR Newswire Knowledge Center (www.prnewswire.com/knowledge-center/): White papers and information on the latest research and PR trends

PRWeb Learning (http://service.prweb.com): Information on new products, technology, and other industry trends

PR Week (www.prweek.com): A news site and magazine for PR professionals

PR Tools (Free and Paid)

Business Wire (www.businesswire.com/portal/site/home/): News release distribution for business and industry

CisionPoint Small Business (http://us.cision.com/products_services/products_services_overview.asp): Public relations software for media lists, news release distribution, media monitoring and analysis

Help a Reporter Out (www.helpareporter.com): A free source for story leads from more than twenty thousand reporters (also follow founder Peter Shankman on Twitter: @skydiver)

Media Kitty (www.mediakitty.com): A service that connects journalists and business professionals "through quick and easy postings," including a Twitter component

PR Newswire (www.prnewswire.com): The oldest and most well known news release distribution service, now with social media distribution as well as traditional media

ProfNet (https://profnet.prnewswire.com/ProfNetHome.aspx): PR Newswire's media lead service, established in 1992, that connects reporters with expert sources

PR Web (www.prweb.com): The news release distribution service owned by Vocus

Vocus SBE (www.vocus.com/content/prsmallbusiness.asp): Media list making, news release distribution, and social media tracking software for sole proprietors and small businesses

Index

About the Author

Randi Minetor started Minetor & Company, Inc., in June 1998, and today her one-woman public relations and writing firm enjoys a client list of leading manufacturing companies in theatrical rigging, municipal water distribution, printing and publishing, computer technology, alternative energy sources, and several other industries. Minetor & Company also serves nonprofit organizations in education, elder care, and land conservation. Often working with her husband, photographer Nic Minetor, Randi has written books in FalconGuides' *National Park Pocket Guides, Best Easy Day Hikes,* and *Passport Companion Guides* series, as well as in GPP's *Timeline Guides* series. The Minetors' first book with Lyons Press, *Backyard Birding: A Guide to Attracting and Identifying Birds,* was released in 2011, and they have recently launched a series of *National Park Quest Guides* as Kindle books. Randi is a professional speaker and has traveled extensively to share her knowledge of public relations, publishing, and professional women's issues with professional association members nationwide.